Dancing with Jesus

Lori Michalina Wood

FLC BUSINESS CONSULTING

Dancing with Jesus / Lori Michalina Wood, 2025

Lovell Casiero, Ed.

Frances Owen, Ed.

ISBN: 979-8-9892004-4-3 (paperback) | 979-8-9892004-5-0 (ebook)

DANCING WITH JESUS

Book cover and design by Frances Owen

Unless otherwise indicated, all Bible passages quoted in this book are from the New International Version (NIV)

Printed in the United States of America

This book is dedicated to

My Heavenly Father, my Lord Jesus Christ, the One who invited me to the dance. He inspired every thought, word, and Scripture in this book. He has shown me true love, and He continues to help me become who I was born to be. All of this is possible all because Jesus loves me.

Contents

Introduction

"Without faith it is impossible to please God." Hebrews 11:6

It was the summer of 2016 when I found myself driving toward the quiet shores of Topsail Island, searching for something I couldn't name—comfort, clarity, healing, maybe even hope. I had no grand plan. I only knew I was being drawn. I could feel the gentle pull of the Holy Spirit urging me toward the water, whispering, "Come away with Me. Let Me show you something."

When I arrived, the pain I carried was unbearable. My heart was shattered by loss and confusion. My mind raced with questions: *Why, God? Why is this happening? What am I doing here? How could this possibly help?* But even louder than the questions was the ache—the deep sorrow that clung to every part of me. Still, I had taken a step. Looking back now, I see how significant that single act was. Sometimes one obedient step toward Jesus is far more powerful than a thousand in any other direction.

That first night, I did what I could to settle in. I unpacked my things through a blur of tears. Panic hovered close, trying to wrap its cold fingers around me, but I reminded myself: *I am tired, I am heartbroken, but I am here. That is enough for now.* I made a simple dinner, and I went to bed, holding tightly to my mother's words: *"Things have a way of looking better in the morning."* She was right, as mothers often are.

The next morning, sunlight poured through the wide ocean-facing window of my bedroom. But it wasn't the brightness of the day that woke me—it was the overwhelming sense of being held. I opened my eyes and knew instantly: I was not alone. I felt wrapped in love, in comfort, in peace that made no earthly sense. It was as if Jesus Himself came into that room and lay beside me, surrounding me with His presence. It was real. I didn't imagine it. He was with me.

He was holding me.

That morning, He spoke—not audibly, but clearly and deeply—through His Word:

"The Lord is close to the brokenhearted and saves those who are crushed in spirit." Psalm 34:18

This book, *Dancing with Jesus*, was born from that sacred moment and the many that followed. It is the continuation of my journey that began in *The Invitation*, where I first shared the gentle tug of God drawing me deeper into our relationship. But this story—this dance—is different. This is about what happens when you say yes to that invitation and then face unimaginable loss. This is about what it looks like to walk with Jesus through heartbreak, and somehow, against all odds, learn to dance again.

This book isn't about having perfect faith or avoiding pain. It's about discovering the rhythm of grace, learning to move even when you're wounded, and trusting the arms that never let you fall. It's about finding Jesus not just in the sanctuary, but in the shattered pieces of life—and discovering that He dances most beautifully with those who are broken.

So, wherever you are—whether you're taking your first trembling step toward healing or just trying to survive another day—I pray this story meets you gently. I pray you feel seen, known, and held.

Because the dance has already begun.

And He is waiting.

Will you join Him?

"Faith is believing a promise, taking God at His Word, believing the Bible to be true, and stepping out upon it."

—J. Dwight Pentecost

His Majesty

I love to walk in my neighborhood in the evening, especially when the sun begins to set, and by the end of my walk, the stars come out. My neighborhood has sidewalks and streetlights, so I feel safe. That evening, I grabbed Bella's leash, my border collie who has walked many miles with me, and we headed out the door. My mind was a bit cluttered that day, and I felt somewhat lost as I left, so I hoped to find peace and solace under the stars.

If we pause, take a moment, and quiet our minds, we will feel the peace of Jesus. His presence is there even in the midst of our chaos, but we must slow down to recognize it.

As I walked down the driveway that evening, there was a beautiful big sky in front of me, with the moon glowing and stars twinkling at me. I thought to myself, "Oh, what a masterpiece of art staring at me." It was an unusual evening as I stood there; even the moon looked a little eerie, but at the same time, it was unbelievably beautiful. It was a perfect September night. I love walking in a tank top and shorts; I enjoy feeling the air brush against my skin. It reminds me that I am alive and well, overcoming the struggles of life. We aren't supposed to walk by feelings, but in this case, it's allowed. What a comforting feeling to know I am on the other side of a storm and confident He is beside me.

It was at that moment that I began a conversation with Jesus, walking along and passing by houses, just wondering what was happening inside each of them. Is it a happy home full of God's peace? Why are the lights off when there are cars in the driveway? It is too early for bedtime. Could they be snuggled under a blanket watching TV with their family, simply happy to be together? During this season of my life, my mind drifts there, and sometimes I know it's not good for me to dwell on these thoughts and create pictures in my mind, but that's where I found myself at that time. A bit of sadness washed over me as I glanced back and saw my house on the hill. A wave of panic can strike you during times of change. Why is that? It's a place you've never been before, and you feel anxious about the future, unsure of what's going to happen. When those thoughts arose from time to time, I leaned even harder into my faith. I turned back around and continued to walk.

Big journeys begin with small steps. I knew that if I was walking with God and trusting in His promises, it would be a journey of peace and healing. God never disappoints! This trust has kept me going as I navigate through the trials and tribulations of my life. In the past, emotions often surfaced during those walks, but tonight, something different happened.

The sadness thickened as I thought about everything around me, but it was only for a moment tonight because, as soon as it arrived, another thought came to me, and I echoed out loud the words I heard. "His Majesty, the King, is all around me. His Majesty, the King, is all around me." Once I heard these words, I knew they were from God. I was taken aback for a moment! I was surprised by what had just come from my lips! It is my faith to believe that God sees everything, and that night, He saw me!

I was quickly reminded of the time I flew on a plane with my kids for the first time when they were little. I'll never forget it. We had boarded the plane and were all excited to visit my parents' home. As the plane took off and we were in the air, I felt just as excited as my kids. There is a kid inside all of us; if we let it resurface more often, we would enjoy life so much more. Jesus said, "Let the little children come to me, and do not hinder them, for the kingdom of heaven belongs to such as these."[1]

I was gazing out the window, amazed by the beauty below. I was reminded of the scripture Isaiah 66:1, "Heaven is my throne and the earth is my footstool." I pondered that for a moment while keeping an eye on my little ones next to me, and I continued my conversation with Him. "Father, if the earth is your footstool, then how big are you?" I immediately heard His voice deep inside me, and He spoke back, "I am all around you."

Hearing Him speak to me in that moment, I began to feel tears welling up in my eyes. I was so touched by the conversation

He and I were having. The people all around me had no idea what I was experiencing, though I would have loved to share it that day with anyone who would listen. God wants us to know this about Him and all His creation. That night, underneath the stars, it was still true: God was all around me.

Walking under the moonlight, there was no need to feel sad, no need to think I was alone, and no need to believe that God was not in control. He is with me, walking with me, and He is completely in control. My walk immediately became sweeter at that moment, my steps felt lighter, and joy was welling up inside me. That is how it feels when we recognize His love for us.

On that beautiful September evening, I began my walk with a cluttered mind and a heart that needed a touch. God showed up and made a difference in my life that evening.

My friend, remember that when you need a touch, a miracle, or healing, God knows your need even before you are aware of it. Psalm 121, a chapter worth memorizing, says, "I lift my eyes to the hills; where does my help come from? My help comes from the Lord, the maker of heaven and earth. He will not let your foot slip; He who watches over you will not slumber."[2] David's words of praise to the Lord are given to us to comfort us in times of trouble. So, in those times when you feel the gray clouds of life closing in around you, just look up and know God sees you and understands your circumstances. Remember, my friend, we are not pursuing God; He is pursuing you.

Do you understand what I'm telling you? The God of the universe desires a relationship with us. John 6:44 says, "No one can come to me unless the Father who sent me draws them, and I will raise them up the last day." Why is God pursuing us? He wants us to walk with Him and dedicate our lives to His service. He created you for a purpose, and He has a plan for you that He doesn't want you to miss while you are here on this earth.

I heard a true story not too long ago about a man who went on a trip, and while he was away, he bought his wife a beautiful, expensive necklace. He was excited to give her this gift when he returned home. He waited for the whole family to gather around before presenting her with the stunning necklace. Naturally, she loved it! She placed it on the table to admire it. As the evening became busy, she went to bed, leaving the necklace on the table, never thinking that it might not be safe in her home.

The next morning, her husband woke up and went to the kitchen to brew coffee. The puppy they were dog-sitting for their children was chewing on something sparkly. His mouth dropped and his countenance fell as he saw what was in the puppy's mouth. This beautiful necklace, which had seemed safe on the table the night before, is now in the puppy's mouth. This puppy didn't understand the value of this lovely necklace; it was just something that looked interesting and perhaps a good chew toy.

If we aren't careful, that may be just how we view our lives. Like the puppy, we often overlook the value we possess and the importance of our purpose here. Psalm 139 explains the intricacies of how God created us. "We were knitted together in our mother's womb and fearfully and wonderfully made."[3]

Knitting requires a great deal of time, and God invested that time into creating you and me. Each day you live on this earth has already been ordained and recorded in the book of life. Your purpose and design were carefully planned. What if we treated our purpose as a valuable piece of "intricately designed jewelry," approaching each day with a mindset of purpose, honoring God, our Father, for He is good!

Often, when you feel downcast and life isn't quite what you expected, you're in the best place ever. I promise you! It's not over! Don't give up; instead, put your faith and trust in Jesus. You won't remain in that low place forever. He is working things out for your good. Trust Him; nothing pleases Him more! It is there in that place that you can look up, literally, and say to the God who created you, "My help comes from you, Lord." Be assured, my friend, I am living proof. He helped me, and He will do the same for you. Trust Him even when it seems dark, because His Majesty, the King, is all around you.

The Misty Lowlands

If you read my first book, *The Invitation: A Love Story*, you may remember the chapter, "The Misty Lowlands." I was first introduced to this phrase by Author A.W. Tozer in his book, *The Pursuit of God*. He described the misty lowlands as a life of defeat and hopelessness; a place not intended for God's children to live. Without guidance, growing up in a negative environment may lead us to believe it is normal. In an environment where insecurity and rejection prevail, the enemy of our soul can do his greatest work. Our young hearts and souls are not mature enough to recognize the trap we become entangled in. We need God's truth to set us free. Unfortunately, it may take years for freedom to arrive.[1]

Genesis 1:27 says, "So God created mankind in his image, in the image of God he created them, male and female." God created us in His Image. Acts 17:26 says, "From one man he made all the nations, that they should inhabit the whole earth;

and he marked out their appointed times in history and the boundaries of their lands." God has placed us exactly where He wanted us and has a purpose in mind as well. If we are made in His image, and we look around at all God has made, we know from the scriptures that the misty lowlands, an environment of insecurity or hopelessness, are not the plan God has for us. He is a mighty God, and He is our Father. We are His offspring. Psalm 93:4 says, "Mightier than the thunders of many waters, mightier than the waves of the sea, the Lord on high is mighty." Reflect on this now that you know we are created in His image!

Chaos erupted in the Garden of Eden when Eve gave in and bit the apple. She believed the serpent's lie that day and took that fateful bite.[2] For many years, I succumbed to the same deception. I accepted the lie that I was not valued, which led me to believe I wasn't good enough either. The enemy worked tirelessly in my heart to convince me of my insignificance, leaving me feeling empty inside. As I reflect on this, I realize the enemy took too much of my time. Thank goodness God is in control and has the final say in all things related to my life.

I will never forget my brother's graduation ceremony many years ago. The speaker delivered a message I will always remember. He spoke to the graduates and the attendees that day, informing us about giants in the land – giants we would encounter as we ventured into the world to find our purpose.

The timing of that message could not have been more perfect for me and my circumstances. I was in my early twenties, trying to figure out why I was here. As we go through our journey, following the plans we have made or making them up as we go, we will encounter giants. What kind of giants? Giants that stay hidden and whisper, but mostly they shout in our ears daily. Giants of abandonment, giants of rejection, giants of fear, and giants of addiction, to name just a few. It will be up to us to recognize them and overcome each one that stands in our way. At some point in everyone's life, we will encounter them, and that is the point the speaker wanted to make.

Most likely, you have heard the Bible story of David slaying Goliath. David fought Goliath (a physical giant) while the whole army of Israel was paralyzed in their boots.[3] The interesting part is that I always viewed this story as a little boy defeating a giant, which in itself was very impressive. What I did not consider was that David, the shepherd boy, came in the name of the Lord. I had read that scripture many times before I realized this aspect of the story. I knew David was highly skilled as a shepherd, protecting his sheep and defeating intruding animals with a slingshot and a rock. David's ability to defeat the giant was due to his complete surrender and reliance on the Lord's help to use his talent and give him the strength to take down the giant. In natural terms, David was no match for the nine-foot giant, but with God, the impossible became possible.

It does not matter how big or intimidating your giant is. You may feel worthless or undervalued. Just remember, you do not stand alone. Yes, David was a skillful young rock thrower and achieved many victories against wild animals that tried to attack his sheep; it was his job as a shepherd to protect them.

That day, standing in front of Goliath was no different; David used his skill, but he relied on God to show up and provide the supernatural power to do the rest. David had one chance to throw the rock; he trusted that God was with him, and he would hit the mark.[4] We are called to trust and believe in the same way David did. YES! You can be that confident.

I am living proof that God will help us bring down the giants in our lives. He will use the smallest talent or skill we possess to amplify our strength. No one can defy God's army, and no one can defy God's child. The question you must ask yourself is, are you turning the battle over to God? Do you believe He will show up like He did for David?

I have learned that when I am facing a giant or perhaps just a negative thought, it can sometimes be as simple as a thought that does not serve me well. I have discovered that if I spend time with the Lord and allow Him to help me work through what is going on inside me, I can find the truth of the matter. Truth changes everything!

I want to share a few words from the Lord on this matter; they will change the rest of your day. Power, love, and a sound mind are ours for the taking. A sound mind is a peaceful mind. Remember this the next time the enemy comes at you. Eve encountered the serpent, but now that Christ has come, our serpent is a serpent without a head. He was defeated at the cross! Yes, Christ defeated all our enemies on the Cross. The devil is powerless if we believe the scriptures, but he can wreak havoc on a mind that does not believe the Word and have faith in God.

I am reminded of a story I heard a young man tell at a kids' camp in South Carolina. One of the jobs at this camp was to watch over the trails to ensure no snakes were lurking around the paths where the children walked. When they came upon a rattlesnake, their instructions were to chop off its head and bury it. Chopping off its head was not enough; the fangs of that snake were still deadly with venom, so it had to be buried. Can you believe that? The fangs of a dead snake are full of poison, enough to be fatal to anyone who steps on them.

The same is true for the lies and thoughts we entertain; they can be fatal to us, too. And like a snake bite, these thoughts can also be paralyzing. The enemy is real, and without God, we are no match. He wants to destroy God's people, and he doesn't care how long it takes. However, when you begin to act as a child of God, you become a threat to the enemy. Did you understand that? When you begin to know who you are in Christ, you have the power to make demons tremble! What is your giant? What lies leave you feeling powerless? What is mocking you or robbing you of a life of peace? What lie has he whispered to you that paralyzes you with fear? Which one have you bought into and believed to be true about you?

Do not let the enemy tell you who you are; neither should you listen to the voices in your head. Allow God and only God to define who you are! In my circumstances, I allowed insecurity and rejection to linger for way too long. I bit the apple early in my childhood. I listened to the lies and believed them. The word "boundary" was one I had never heard, and my world did not feel safe. Rejection set me up so many times, only to let me fall flat on my face. It was hard; it was painful. The enemy also uses others in your life to play his games. His trickery is fueled by deception. The people he uses do not even realize they are pawns, and we are so distracted by the battle that we don't even see ourselves being set up. Unhealthy people are everywhere, and pain and suffering are a part of life, but right in the middle of it all, God calls us overcomers. That's right, you are an overcomer! That is the good news I came to share with you! Christ came to set the captive free! That is why He came to the earth, knowing He would die in order to redeem the world from original sin.

Goliath fell that day, and his head was chopped off as David took the sword Goliath carried in his sheath and beheaded him.[5] Yes, that's right; the enemy was decapitated by his own sword. The enemy would love to keep you imprisoned in your heart and soul until you leave this world. I can't bear to think that someone may need this truth and not have it. Friend, if there is a giant with its foot on your neck, trust and believe that God can turn your situation around. You can find glory in your situation.

It wasn't long ago that I found myself in one of those struggles and became entangled in them when I heard my Father say to me, "When His Word (our blueprint) in me is louder than the enemy's words, then you will overcome and begin to rise from these ashes to fulfill your highest calling."

Hear what I am saying: truth is your greatest weapon! His Word in your life daily, and using the message to resist the enemy, is how we rise above it. God rescued me from the pit, and He wants to rescue you, too. How do you know if you are in a pit? Look around and see if it resembles the misty lowlands. Do you feel safe? Do you feel hopeless? Is there a giant in your life? Answer those questions truthfully, because we must be responsible for what we allow into our lives. Psalm 18:2 says, "The Lord is my Rock, my fortress and my deliverer; my God is my rock, in whom I take refuge, my shield and the horn of my salvation, my stronghold." Further, Psalm 18:4-5 says, "The cords of death entangled me; the torrents of destruction overwhelmed me; the snares of death confronted me. In my distress I called to the Lord; I cried to my God for help. From His temple He heard my voice; my cry came before Him, into His ears."

The scriptures are there for us. If you need to print them out and paste them in front of you to remember this promise, then do it! God's word teaches us to resist the devil, and he will flee. Psalm 44:5: "Through you, we push back our enemies; through your name, we trample our foes. I put no trust in my bow, my sword does not bring me my victory, but you give us victory over our enemies; you put our adversaries to shame."

Jesus, my deliverer and Savior, is the hero of my journey, and all it took was my surrender to Him. It feels like a dance! Just surrender and believe! All I did was trust His Word and declare it. When I'm lying in bed, feeling troubled or surrounded by the lingering effects of past lies, I start quoting what I know from His Word. His Word is alive! Psalm 23 always brings me peace. I can relax and enjoy sweet sleep as I recite every line of that Psalm.

David said, "In God, we make our boast all day long, and we will praise your name forever." I'm sure he celebrated his deliverer on the day he defeated Goliath, paving the way for his future encounters with giants. He understood he wasn't alone, and his God was a powerful warrior. Our Father wishes to empower us against the giants we face. Do you feel powerless against the enemy? Has he whispered in your ear that you stand no chance, that it's too late, that you're too old, or that you will never be healed? Have you succumbed to the lie that God doesn't notice you? That is precisely what the enemy desires. Open the Word of God and begin declaring! It's never too late! You can confront that adversary by saying, "Do you know who I serve? Do you know who fights for me?" God will stand right by you on the battlefield!

In 2016, I lost my dad to suicide, and the Lord gave me the song "The Misty Lowlands" right before it all happened. I wrote this song as if it were a letter my heavenly Father was dictating to me from Heaven. The Lord loves to send us messages and will use all kinds of ways to do so. On that day, He used my voice and my guitar. As I sat on my bed one afternoon, these were the words that came to me.

"The Misty Lowlands"

I hear a voice calling me, out into the deep, a place I've never been before, it's dark and I can't see. I've walked with Him so many times, I know, and I believe, that He wouldn't call me here if it wasn't for my good, you see."

I am tired of the misty lowlands; I am tired of defeat, and I know I was created with purpose in me. I have to take this step of faith, step out of this boat; no longer can I stay here; something tells me I must go.

So, I listened to His voice, I hear Him speak to my soul; rise up, my fair one, you're with me and you will know. Every step I will meet you, my Grace will be there too, and you will see how I will care for you in the deep too.

Though the wind be raging and the voices, too; keep your eyes on me, I'm in front of you.

He intended to call me out into the depths. In the dark, deep waters is where Jesus walks; clouds form the paths He travels, rendering storms powerless against Him. I was unaware that the words I was writing would become my reality that year. His daughter was meant for more than just the lowlands; He envisioned higher places for me to explore. The challenge was that I was so entrenched in a pit that escaping those lowlands would require significant effort before I could ever envision a higher destination.

Have you ever experienced these feelings? It reminds me of Moses arguing with God because he felt he could not face Pharaoh (the giant of intimidation). Moses was instructed by God to lead the children of Israel out of Egypt. He was explaining to God that He had picked the wrong man. His excuse was that he was unqualified, but it didn't matter because God had chosen him. Moses led the children of Israel out of Egypt, and his brother Aaron came with him. Moses had been in the desert for forty years; so, when God spoke to him through the burning bush to go and free his people, Moses felt unqualified.[6]

On the same day, God inspired me with the second verse of "The Misty Lowlands," and it wasn't long before I began walking it out. God acts, and in the 77th Chapter of Psalms, David describes how it may feel when God starts to move. Perhaps you're experiencing something similar right now. "The waters saw you, O God, the waters twisted; the very depths were convulsed. The clouds poured down water, the skies resounded with thunder; your arrows flashed back and forth. Your thunder was heard in the whirlwind; your lightning lit up the world; the earth trembled and quaked. Your path led through the sea, your way through the mighty waters, though your footprints were not seen. You led your people like a flock by the hand of Moses and Aaron."[7]

I recall feeling as though He was guiding me when I stepped out of the boat onto the vast waters. Leaving a place of comfort and security, where I had spent so much time, I was now being asked to trust Him enough to walk on water. My surroundings resembled the scriptures I had just shared, and that was precisely what Jesus intended. God was calling me, saying, "Get up and step out and come to Me." The Invitation, my own story, took place on the shores of Topsail, North Carolina, where Jesus beckoned me. God knows the perfect moment to invite you to come. There would be no footprints visible—just complete trust, as He walks on clouds. I vividly remember the weather during that season of my life, especially that day on the shoreline. Physical storms were also present that day. I recall the dark clouds and lightning illuminating the sky night after night for an extended period. Yet, I had encountered those verses, and I understood that God was at work. It was both fearsome and humbling. I remember the earth trembling; I couldn't see any footprints, but I trusted God knew the path, and I was meant to keep my eyes on Him as I continued walking. It was truly a humbling experience. I approached Him, bringing all the broken pieces of my life's shattered moments.

The death of my father shattered me. I loved him deeply and wanted to see him overcome the giants in his life. I tried so hard to help him. Following this tragic time, the death of my marriage came within a few months. After twenty-seven years of striving to make the relationship work, I felt broken once more. I felt like Cinderella, held captive in a tower – a tower of grief. It was then that God stepped in and invited me to take His hand. He sees everything; the pieces of me that were left at the feet of Jesus, and He took them. Jesus wanted them, and He knew He would use them in my journey of healing.

All your pain, grief, self-loathing, disappointments, abuse, and regrets will not be in vain. I assure you, if you step out of that boat, walk on the waters, and focus on Jesus, you won't be let down. Psalm 18:16-19 reassures us: "He reached down from on high and took hold of me; He drew me out of the deep waters. He rescued me from my powerful enemy, who was too strong for me. They confronted me on the day of my disaster, but the Lord was my support." Such immense love He has for us.

While cleaning my closet one day, a piece of paper fell from a book on a high shelf and floated down to the floor. The words on it read, "He brought me out into a spacious place; He rescued me because He delighted in me."[8] It was yet another beautiful reminder from Him, a message from Heaven reassuring me that He is in control of my life and managing everything. How amazing is that! It wasn't a coincidence; my loving Father, in His miraculous ways, made it possible for that slip of paper to fall from the book and come to my attention.

Messages and words from our Father are everywhere. He isn't hiding from us; rather, He is waiting to be seen by us. I will never forget that moment in the closet when He let me know everything would be alright! That would be the title of the next song He gave me. The words of that song describe a little girl seeking love, while her Heavenly Father keeps a close eye on her as she navigates through life. It would be then, in the ashes, that she would look up and discover God was there, ready to help her rise from the ashes of these misty lowlands. I didn't know it yet, but the ashes would become beautiful, mourning would turn to joy, and that grave would become beautiful gardens for her. It was something I couldn't do, but I knew He could, so I was determined to keep walking.

To feel like Daddy's little girl was all I ever wanted, and now I am God's little girl, and all the wrong is turning into right. What comfort to find that I was Daddy's little girl all along.

The misty lowlands are not your home either, so don't settle for a pit when Jesus came and died on a cross for you. Surrender your life and dance with Him. Surrendering is not about giving up something; that is how we look at it. Surrender is about giving Him control over all the negativity and baggage you have been holding on to. Surrender is about coming home to your Father and allowing Him to show you the plan He has for you, committing to take one step at a time, one day at a time.

Rich treasures and value are sown into your very core; an intricately designed precious jewel lies within you. Jesus knows it's there, and He wants you to recognize it. He wants to bring you up to the dance floor; He wants you to be whole. He wants you to shine!

So, my friend, consider those dance shoes you're holding. Follow wherever He guides you, maintain trust even when the path is unclear, and listen to me when I tell you not to worry; your life isn't over. He will save you. Have faith and put on your dancing shoes. They might take a bit of time to get used to, but they were handmade specifically for you. Ask yourself today: misty lowlands or the ball? Cinderella chose the ball, and she stood out as the most beautiful young lady there, ultimately finding her prince that night. Are you ready to go to the ball?

The Dance Floor

Have you ever had the chance to take a dance lesson or watch a couple dancing on the dance floor? A movie that comes to my mind is "Shall We Dance."[1] It is a wonderful film. I love music and dancing, but the only dancing I have mastered is in my kitchen. I enjoy watching couples dance, and I occasionally tune in to "Dancing with the Stars"[2] on television. The dance floor is what stands out to me most; that's where it all happens. The ambiance, lights, and the beautiful wide-open space where we see music come to life through dance. It's that moment when a couple walks hand in hand to the center of the dance floor, pauses, turns, and looks at each other while waiting for the music to begin. Just imagine their hearts beating and their nerves as they await the start of the music.

As you can imagine that scene, go a little further with me and picture yourself there. Close your eyes and see yourself stepping onto the dance floor, walking to the center under the lights as you wait for your partner. Can you recall a time in your life when you sat by a dance floor, hoping someone would ask you to dance? I remember it, and I'm sure, like me, you've stood beside the dance floor wanting to dance, but too shy to ask. Maybe it was your high school prom. You were all dressed up, hoping for a dance with that special someone.

I am reminded of another movie I love, "Footloose."[3] Think of the scene where young teens sit around a dance floor, too afraid to dance. The film portrays a conservative town that forbids dancing until a newcomer arrives, eager to change their mindset. A town meeting was held, and Kevin Bacon, the actor, was ready to rise to the occasion. To make an impact, he needed to sway the local pastor, a highly influential man in the town; Bacon turned to the scriptures for support. It was a priceless moment. He approached the podium and started reading from Ecclesiastes, specifically the third chapter. King Solomon, the author, penned such a thought-provoking book. The scripture provides perspective, and that night, it resonated perfectly with Kevin Bacon.

Bacon began to read Ecclesiastes 3:1-4: "A time to be born and a time to die, a time to plant and a time to uproot. A time to kill and a time to heal, a time to tear down and a time to build. A time to weep and a time to laugh, a time to mourn and a time to dance."[4] After the townspeople heard these words, they looked at each other, thinking that even the Bible says there is a time to dance. With the support of all his friends, Bacon had convinced the town to let them dance. The next scene shows the two main characters of the movie, Bacon and his girlfriend, walking hand in hand through the doors of the dance hall and leading their friends onto the dance floor. They were thrilled to be dancing that night, eager to express themselves through dance. It was all they wanted.

Now, returning to the dance floor, you have gathered the courage to step onto it. How brave you are! Jesus serves as your dance partner, having uniquely choreographed a dance for you! Did you know there was a special song just for you? Psalm 37:23 states, "The steps of a man are ordered by the Lord who takes delight in his journey." This marks the moment when we experience the dance of our lives. Take a deep breath, as everything depends on your response. He calls us and invites us to join Him—to come and dance; ultimately, the choice is ours.

As I mentioned earlier, I wouldn't consider myself a dancer unless I'm alone in the kitchen with music echoing off the walls. Then, I'm dancing with abandon! That said, I haven't had any formal training when stepping onto a real dance floor. Jesus is enlightening me about dancing with Him, which is a completely different experience than what I'm trying to achieve in my kitchen. He recognized the need to share an experience with me that would give me some idea of what he was asking of me.

This is how Jesus revealed it to me. I was on my way to the horse barn, a wonderful spot where I ride Rocky, a beautiful and majestic horse. I've been fortunate to have a few special friends who share their horses with me, and I truly appreciate their friendship and the chance to ride such incredible horses.

The barn is filled with beautiful horses and wonderful people who love spending time with them. It covers about 100 acres of pastures, trails, barns, and a pond. What I love the most is seeing horses all around. God provides! This place is a dream come true for horse lovers! That's just the kind of Father we have; He wants you to be happy!

I had just started riding Rocky that day. A gift from God, this gentle giant is the sweetest! See, this is how it works! If God knows you need to ride and you don't own a horse, He is capable of going before you and making it happen. He always knows what you need, and His timing is always perfect!

Rocky was an amazing horse; he was grounded in who he was, and frankly, nothing moved him. God was going to teach me some things through Rocky. One day, while riding through the woods, it was quiet, and we were strolling along the path when, out of nowhere, four deer came running across our path. It was the most amazing scene I had ever encountered in the woods; but Rocky, well, he didn't miss a step. If you know anything about horses, then you understand just how good a horse Rocky was because any other horse that day would have given you a ride you would never forget – and hopefully, you lived to talk about it. Rocky wasn't concerned about those deer crossing in front of him, as long as they left him plenty of room to carry me through. I didn't feel a twinge from him, nor was he startled, and to tell you the truth, I didn't know what was more amazing: the deer scene that left me speechless or Rocky's calm behavior. The scene in the woods made me laugh so much, and I let Rocky know how much I appreciated him too.

A beautiful horse named Rocky taught me a lot that day. My dad's death weighed heavily on my heart. It had only been a few months, and so many unanswered questions left me perplexed. It is crucial for us to trust God, remain calm, and hand over those questions to Him. In time, He will answer them and bring you peace. Rocky's calm demeanor that day spoke volumes to my heart. The message I received from the experience was to keep calm and carry on. Yes, God used a horse to speak to me that day, and the message resonated deeply within my soul. "Be still and know that I am God."[5] By listening and staying in communion with the Father, He is also speaking to you.

The Father decided to give me another lesson on a different day. I saddled up Rocky and rode him in the riding ring for a while, but his favorite was the trails, so we headed out for a trail ride. I don't know what prompted me to choose a different direction that day; I ventured out on a trail we hadn't explored before, but I thought I would take a new path. I felt adventurous.

Rocky did whatever I asked, so I had no qualms about him. Off we went, and I was enjoying this beautiful new trail through the woods, soaking in the quiet time. You know, quiet time spent doing something you enjoy is often what God uses to heal your soul. Physically, I was being carried through the woods on Rocky, but he was also leading me through a deep valley. I knew my healing had begun, and it started when I began going to the barn weekly to ride Rocky. The trails in the woods became a place to weep as He carried me through them. Each week as I rode, it reminded me of when I was young and rode all over the countryside on my horse, Sarge.

It's interesting how sometimes God brings us full circle, allowing us to enjoy the things we once did as kids. God led me then on the quiet trails to soothe my soul, and He was guiding me back to them years later. Now, I'm on this trail with Rocky, perhaps having lost track of the passing time. Soon, I notice that it's getting dark, and I'm starting to feel a little anxious. I see no end in sight on this new and unfamiliar path, and I realize I'm deep in the forest. I had been riding and, lost in my thoughts, forgot that the sun was going down. The only thing that came to mind as I heard Rocky's footsteps was the scene from the movie, "The Wizard of Oz." "Lions and tigers and bears, oh my, lions and tigers and bears, oh my."[6] I just wish I felt as cheerful and brave as I did when I sat in front of the TV screen watching that movie as a kid, but this was a very different feeling. I was getting as nervous as the cowardly lion.

I started considering my options. I could turn back and go the way I came, but the problem is that it's getting dark now, and I might be too deep in the forest to make it back to the barn before night falls. Another thought I had was that I could sit tight on this horse, be brave, and see where this path takes me. I have only about five minutes to decide one way or the other because the sun isn't standing still like it did for Joshua that day in the Bible.[7] All the "what ifs" start hitting me, one after the other, and I am forced to make a choice. Am I going to be scared, or am I going to trust that spontaneous decision I made at the beginning of this trail ride to be adventurous?

I reasoned through a thought that led me to the decision I made. I knew the path was on the farm, and maybe it was just a new path I had never taken before. If I could be brave, perhaps I might learn something. It took everything I could muster; I had to dig deep into the core of who I am and search for my sense of adventure from my youth, wondering if it was still there. I made my decision – there's no turning back now. I will take this dark path and see where it leads me and Rocky. As I continued, it was not a quiet ride; I could actually hear my own heartbeat pounding outside my chest! It's funny when we look back at ourselves, but in that moment, there was nothing funny about it.

You wouldn't believe it, but just a little further, around the bend, I began to see green pastures. Oh, my goodness! I had never been so glad to see a green pasture. I didn't even care whose pasture it was; I was just relieved to get out of those woods! God spared the sunlight long enough for me to realize I had emerged onto an open field, and I was just on the other side of the farm. It was a part of the farm I had never seen before, but now I had my bearings back, and so did Rocky. His instincts told him we weren't far from the barn. I let out perhaps the biggest sigh of relief ever, and let me tell you, I was so happy to see a familiar place again.

I share these two amazing experiences with you because it's what Jesus wanted me to understand that day. It was a test! Life on the dance floor with Him is just like that! We can be thrilled with adventure while also being at peace; at other times, we may be living on the edge. We might be taking risks, and the lesson here is that if we're not, we are not truly living! Oh, what a wonderful Savior we have; Jesus wants us to live. He also wants us to trust Him and follow Him through a valley – or in my case, the woods – even if it's a little dark. He will lead us to green pastures. He will guide us to the other side! He wants that for you and me!

Oh, my friend, I don't know about you, but for me, I must confess that sometimes it is hard to trust. Just like it was scary on that dark trail with Rocky, God allowed that moment to show me and teach me that dancing with Jesus can be hard, especially at first. It's okay to feel nervous about the dance, but I encourage you to step out and trust what you know. He wanted me to experience that faith-over-fear moment so I would always remember that if I keep dancing, I will reach green pastures soon enough.

Another teachable moment I want to share with you is about shepherding. I believe we can apply this concept on the dance floor as well. On the dance floor, one partner leads while the other follows, and Jesus is our shepherd, guiding us. As I have studied the scriptures and conducted my research, I have found that the shepherd, when leading his flock, always guides them through the valley to reach the mountains. It's where the grass is abundant and the fresh waters flow; the valley leads us to the mountains. The shepherd is directing his flock to a tableland; another term is mesa, a Spanish word that describes a land formation resembling a table.[8] Before the shepherd takes his flock, he has already gone ahead to clear the area of any dangerous weeds or plants and surveys the land to ensure it is a safe environment for his sheep.

Our good shepherd, Jesus, does the same for us. As parents, we would never say yes to everything our child asks for. This is because we love them, and we know it would not be good for them. The good Shepherd acts in the same way. Psalm 23:5 calls it a table that He prepares for us. Psalm 18:19 says, "He brought me out into a spacious place; he rescued me because He delighted in me." I have a framed picture of Psalm 119:32 decorating a wall in my house, which states, "I will run in the paths of your commands, for you have set my heart free." Another translation says, "I will run after you with delight in my heart, for you will make me obedient to your instructions."

God desires to walk with you and prepare your heart, but you must humble yourself. We must become like children to enter the Kingdom of God; we must obey Him.[9] When He says no and closes a door to something we think we need, we should accept His decision as what is best for us. That's the choreography of the dance; Jesus leads, and we follow. The Word will guide you in whatever situation you find yourself. He created you with a unique personality; He knows you. He will speak differently to each of His children. He knows how to reach you, and you will recognize His voice. His Grace is sufficient for thee.[10]

You are never dancing alone, and that's a promise. Paths of freedom, joy, and great delight await you on the dance floor of life with Jesus. Hebrews 6:15 tells of Abraham, who, after waiting patiently, received what was promised. I want to receive what was promised to me. I want you to receive what God has for you as well.

Are you ready? It's your time! The dance floor is open, and your song is about to play. I have found peace in my dance with Jesus. What about you? Are you ready to take His hand on the dance floor? Don't be afraid; trust Him. Start singing and praising right in the middle of your storm. Oh yes, God loves to see faith like that! God has created everything within you to fulfill your destiny, so when Jesus extends His hand to you, don't think about it; don't hesitate, just dance!

You Belong to Me

Dean Martin, one of the most iconic and talented entertainers, performs a song titled "You Belong to Me." Have you ever listened to it? The song tells the story of a woman who travels internationally, yet wherever she goes, the hook line always reminds her that "she belongs to him." She explores a tropical island and the Pyramids of the Nile; she travels to many places, but he reminds her, "Just remember darling all the while, you belong to me."[1] I will always remember the first time I heard this song playing at an outdoor market while I was shopping. Before that night, I had never heard this song, and as I went in and out of the stores, listening to the music and Dean Martin's voice, I stopped in my tracks because I began to pick up on the lyrics. I believe lyrics of songs are messages, and that evening under the stars, the lyrics came to me that I believe God was singing over me.

It's important to understand who I am. I live by faith, walk by faith, and speak to my Father like I'm His little girl because I've made a wonderful discovery. I truly am His little girl! Though it took me a while, a long while, after discovering this truth, my life has been forever changed. He is pursuing us, my friend. He isn't hiding from us or holding a hammer over us to correct us when we get out of line. No, He is waiting for us to recognize His love for His children. If we adjust our spiritual antennae and become attuned to His Presence, I believe we would be astonished.

I needed that song when I was shopping; I needed to know without a doubt that I belonged to Him. Everyone wants to belong. Sometimes, the struggle of rejection sits right on my shoulder, and my Father knows it. That night, under the stars, He spoke to me through a song. Sadly, rejection has been a giant in my life for as long as I can remember, and disentangling from that mindset takes time; His timing and message that night were perfect! I was touched as I listened to that song and those words: You belong to me. It was the beginning of understanding that I am loved, and I do belong.

I found some interesting scientific facts about God's love in a book I'm reading called *Switch on Your Brain* by Dr. Caroline Leaf, a communication pathologist, audiologist, and clinical neuroscientist. Most importantly, Dr. Leaf is a Christian and has brought to light information concerning an important truth. She writes in her book that the difference in healing for those with HIV was their choice to believe in a benevolent and loving God, especially if they also chose to have a personal relationship with a benevolent and loving God. The study was conducted over four years and found that significant healing was based on the number of helper T-cells in the body. The higher the concentration of these cells, the more effectively the body was able to fight disease. She found that those who did not believe God loved them had fewer helper T-cells, and their viral load increased three times faster. Additionally, their stress levels were higher.[2] What are the facts this study is revealing? If you believe God loves you, it's an enormous protective factor, even more protective than scoring low for depression or high for optimism. She summarizes this study by stating that a view of a benevolent God is protective, but scoring high on the personalized statement "God loves me" is even stronger. We can choose or not choose. God made us so extraordinary that our choices can impact our brain images, which in turn influence our mental and physical health.

Have you noticed how a child listens intently while you read a story to them? Especially when it's their favorite book and they are truly engaged. Their little minds imagine everything as you read. They believe whatever you say, and their faces light up with fascination. Grown-ups are supposed to be like that! I ask you, when was the last time you read the Word of God and felt your eyes light up with fascination?

I believe that narrative is the heartbeat of my book! I enjoy God and want to glorify Him, but I long to share my passion for Him with you. Each morning when I wake up and hear a song playing over and over in my head, I thank Him because I know it's from Him. It's a personal message for me carried on the tune of a song. It is pure inspiration, and those days are among my best writing days. All the inspiration, in whatever form, trickles down from Him. The Word of God says, if I don't come as a child, I cannot inherit the Kingdom of God.[3] I believe that because our childlike faith is all grown up, we rob ourselves of many blessings. Isaiah 9:6 says, "For unto us a child is given, and the government shall be upon His shoulder. The Kingdom of God, my friend, is righteousness, peace, and joy.

Do you have that? It's a daily question you should ask yourself. Every kingdom has a king, with a territory, citizens, laws, and an army that stands guard at every station to protect that kingdom. When you receive Jesus as your Savior, you gain access to the keys to His kingdom, in addition to righteousness, peace, and joy! These are beautiful gifts of salvation. Isaiah 33:6 teaches, "He will be the sure foundation for your times, a rich store of salvation and wisdom and knowledge; the fear of the Lord is the key to this treasure." God didn't send us here to navigate life alone; He has a storehouse of blessings.

One evening, I found myself in one of those life situations that I couldn't figure out alone. I was praying and seeking answers. For a moment, I even thought, "I'm going to call my mom." I hadn't had a thought like that in years. Sure, I wished I could call her, but this was different. I felt a real urge to call, and for a split second, I forgot that she was no longer here. Calling her in the natural sense was impossible. I was that perplexed by my situation, and that's just how life is sometimes. It wraps us up like a suffocating blanket, and if we didn't know God, we would act out and fall apart. Then I had a second thought: to call a friend who was a little mother hen to me. I believed the Lord sent her into my life after losing my mother. That is how God works, always looking out for His children. My friend's name is Doris. The problem was I didn't call Doris; I got busy and forgot. I continued to pray all afternoon for help and seek answers from the Lord. My situation wasn't changing, and time was ticking away. My help had to come soon, or I wouldn't sleep at all that night.

Later that evening, I sat down and turned my Bible to the bookmark that held my place in Isaiah 33:6: "He will be the sure foundation for your times, a rich storehouse of salvation and wisdom and knowledge; the fear of the Lord is the key to this treasure." Yes, I was going to the storehouse because I needed wisdom. I intended to take God at His Word and explore this for myself. I meditated on this promise and began to express gratitude for the answer I had not yet received. When I closed my Bible, I picked up my guitar and worshipped through song. The song I chose to sing was "Have Thine Own Way, Lord." How appropriate, I thought to myself; I wanted to let God know that I understood. "Thou art the potter and I am the clay."[4] I sang that song over and over, and the words and melody began to heal me. I started to feel better about things.

Worship will always settle and bring peace to your heart. It looks different for everyone because we are all so unique. It may not change a circumstance, but it will change you to better cope with the circumstances.

Later that evening, I received a phone call. No coincidence, it was Doris! Since I hadn't called her, she was calling me. She said that I had been on her heart all day, and she would not be able to sleep that night if she didn't check on me. That's just the kind of loving friend she is. We sat and talked for as long as it took for her to share her wisdom with me about the things I needed that evening.

So, you see, my friend, how God is always near, watching over us. I told Doris she was an answer to my prayer that day. Sometimes God speaks directly, and at other times He speaks through another person. Always remember, when you are in a dilemma, lay your request at the feet of Jesus, turn your attention to the Word, and begin to worship Him for what He is going to do! Go to the storehouse! There's salvation, wisdom, and knowledge waiting for you in abundance, and God's storehouse never runs out!

Just this morning, as I was reading a book about rejection, I realized God wanted me to understand certain things. There are likely many levels of rejection, but rejection by a parent or a spouse can shape how we view ourselves for a lifetime, if we allow it. A lack of words and affection from a dad can be debilitating, and harsh words spoken by anyone we love can feel like arrows in our souls – but again, only if we allow it. Rejection is a giant that can host a party in your soul, bringing along friends named insecurity, inferiority, guilt, perfectionism, and pain. How can you deal with it? How can you rid your mind of those toxic thoughts? Turn to Jesus and believe every Word that He says about you and the life you were predestined to have, and receive His promises and acceptance. Yes, Jesus accepts you. We belong to Him!

Have you ever created something that made you feel incredibly proud? I sometimes strive to create, and I have succeeded in making various things. One of the crafts I am most proud of is the window treatments I made for my house. I must say they are absolutely beautiful, and no one could convince me otherwise. As mothers, we hold one of life's greatest honors. We carry our children for nine months as God knits them together in our wombs, and when the time comes, we endure significant pain to deliver them and introduce them to this world. Yes, being a mother has been my greatest fulfillment. I am blessed to have four unique, sweet, loving, and amazing boys. I could go on and on about them! Nothing like the fury of a mother's love, and rightly so, because I would go to the ends of the earth for mine! I love them and want them to know it.

That's how our Father feels about His children, and He looks for every opportunity to let us know it. You will have to walk by faith, and the struggle will be there, but it's only because you are changing a lie that you have believed for a long time about yourself. During this process, you will need to give yourself grace. Consider the journey as a newly planted little tree. It is a fresh start for this young sprout. It will require nurturing and care until it grows stronger. This simple analogy helped me allow myself more grace in my journey. I grew up feeling invaluable, and changing that mindset takes time and often comes with tears. I still occasionally stumble over this lie; the enemy never gives up. But now I know I am valuable and important to God and others.

I've heard a saying that holds a lot of truth. You may have heard it too: rejected people reject others. Hurt people hurt others. Break the cycle of injury; let it start with you. Don't allow it any more life. Take a moment to look back at the generations that have passed, and perhaps you will see how that cycle has persisted in your family. It certainly was in my family. By stopping it and changing your mindset, along with how you think about yourself, you will impact not only yourself, but you will also change the course of your family tree. Yes, it can happen!

Studies show that the good, the bad, and the ugly do pass down through generations, but your mind is the signal. You can impact these genes simply by adopting a new way of behaving. It is fascinating; once you grasp this truth, you will be a walking miracle, and in time, you will know it. God can remove that awful lie and fill you with joy. You can be the difference in someone's life without even realizing it. Remember, the most important thing you can do for your healing is to accept yourself, love yourself, and take care of you! You are like no other! You are unique, you are loved, and you have a purpose.

Brené Brown, a gifted writer and speaker, has written many books on the subject of belonging. *Braving the Wilderness* is one of my favorites. I wanted to read it to discover her insights about belonging. In her book, she discusses the power of vulnerability, the quest for true belonging, and the courage to stand alone.[5] Oh, I wanted all of that! It's a wilderness experience we wander into, and we can emerge different on the other side. Isn't that what everyone truly wants? To see ourselves in a way we never have before. She talks about Jacob in the Bible and the wilderness experience he faced. Jacob entered the wilderness due to a dishonest act against his brother, Esau. His brother was furious, and Jacob walked away. Jacob had tricked him and stolen his birthright; he was afraid. But God saw it! One night, Jacob fell asleep in the desert and woke up to find himself wrestling with God. He longed for a blessing from God! Was it a dream? Was it a vision? What was it? It doesn't matter. The important thing is that Jacob emerged from the experience a changed man. From that struggle, Jacob received a blessing; he got a new name. As a reminder of the struggle, he walked with a limp for the rest of his life, but most importantly, he knew that God was there that night. After tricking his brother and stealing his birthright, he still belonged to God. That was all Jacob needed to know!

After reading *Braving the Wilderness*, I discovered a valuable truth: braving the wilderness will, in time, give you a strong back to lead, a soft front of compassion, and a wild heart. A heart to live, to dance, to create, and to thrive because it has been touched and forever changed. When we know we belong to God, we can then walk in our uniqueness, walk in our purpose, and walk with courage. You may come away with a limp; you may not come through unscathed, but you will come through changed! You will wrestle with yourself at times, and the battle will be real. The enemy will work hard to remind you of the lies you embraced all your life; it may sometimes come out of nowhere. That is when you must take your stand.

I had this occurrence just the other day. I resisted the devil and the thoughts he was bringing to me all day, and then I remembered a scripture: Isaiah 54:17, "No weapon formed against me will prosper." I want to be clear with you that it is a battle. The weapons he uses and his tactics are going to strike you and feel like an arrow, but the scripture I am sharing is powerful. "No weapon formed against you will prosper." You can use this scripture to remind the enemy of his lack of power over you, and it will subside. Speak the Word over it! One day you will have the chance to bring hope to others and share your testimony of how you overcame. Your scars will inspire hope in others, and that's what it is all about.

I was walking under the stars one night, just talking to the Father about what was on my heart. I shared with Him how, as a woman, it's nice to have someone look at us and smile or give us a nice compliment. We don't even need someone special in our lives; it's just nice to be noticed. I heard Him speak right back to my heart and say, "You don't even need that, because I notice you all the time and you have my attention always." Well, I wasn't expecting that, but it sure made me think. I was completely astonished by His Word, and my heart swelled that night. My Heavenly Father, Almighty God, is taking notice of me and affirms me in His Word and sings over me continually; and that is all the attention I need. I received it that night, right under the stars. God is right! We have been accepted already! That will knock the wind right out of that giant called rejection. It will make him take his friends and go home.

Let me share something funny that left me smiling. As soon as I came home that evening from my walk, I decided to play some music on my phone. I turned on Pandora, specifically the Dean Martin station, and God just lit up my phone. The very next song that played was "You Belong to Me." That's right! God will send an extra message because He is an extra, extra good Father!

Let me leave you with a few lyrics from the song I have been sharing in this chapter: "Fly the ocean in a silver plane, see the jungle when it's wet with rain, just remember 'til you're home again, you belong to me."[6]

God is pursuing you, and He will work hard to make you feel noticed; you always have His attention. You don't want anyone to take the place that God desires. Let Him be your first love, and when the time is right, He will bring you the desires of your heart. Why does He do this? Because... you belong to Him!

***

The Man in the Arena

It is not the critic who counts, not the man who points out how the strong man stumbles, or where the doer of deeds could have done them better. The credit belongs to the man who is actually in the arena, whose face is marred by dust and sweat and blood, who strives valiantly...... who knows great enthusiasms, the great devotions, who spends himself in a worthy cause, who at the best knows in the end the triumph of high achievement, and who at the worst, if he fails, at least fails while daring greatly, so that his place shall never be with those cold and timid souls who neither know victory nor defeat.

~ Teddy Roosevelt

Dancing with Jesus

I wish I could recall the exact moment Jesus invited me to dance with Him. However, I will never forget the moment He asked me to come out to the deep with Him on the shores of Topsail Island. As I stood at the water's edge, staring out into the deep, I could feel Him extending His hand and inviting me to come. Deep water scares me. So, of all the places where the Lord could have extended His hand to me, it was the place I feared the most. Nevertheless, like the disciple Peter, I wanted to follow Jesus wherever He was leading.

In the fall of 2016, a painful year for me, I wrote the song "I Want to Dance with You Jesus." Day after day, those words continued to play on a continuous loop in my mind. I visualized myself and Jesus on the dance floor. One day, as those words kept repeating in my thoughts, I picked up my guitar and began to put words to what I was feeling, writing the lyrics of this new song that resonated in my heart.

The first verse came quickly, "Lord, I sense you calling me to the dance floor, but I've never danced before, yet you don't seem to mind. You tell me to just follow and keep your eyes on me."

I remember my heart beating faster than I could put these words on paper. I know my inspiration always comes from Jesus. He knew I was hurting and was comforting me through the lyrics of this song. It was lifting me up. Jesus and I both understood that my soul needed healing, and I truly desired to be all He created me to be. I was deep in the valley, and I realized I needed help. He knew it too!

I heard this quote the other day; it's an excerpt from the book *Captivating* by John and Stasi Eldredge. "You must live the life you were born to live."[1] Wow, I thought to myself! That quote almost haunted me the first time I read it. I can't miss the life I was born to live! I certainly don't want to miss it. I must trust Him with the plan. We each have a purpose that God has placed deep within us since the beginning, when He created us. He formed and fashioned us, and we must trust God's plan. We must say yes to His invitation. If not, we will miss the purpose God has for us.

I truly believe that the Lord spoke to me about dancing with Him, offering a different perspective on my journey. Let's face it, we all go through the valley. I am certain that in the valley is where the Lord is teaching us something. We are never alone in the valley; Jesus is always walking with us.

For me, Jesus was trying to paint a picture of a couple on a dance floor. He wanted me to see that He was there with me in my pain and confusion and present in the valley – the valley I wasn't supposed to be in. Remember, in the valley, you are only passing through. A more comforting thought is knowing you are in the arms of Jesus as you go through your valley. This is where the dance starts. You know, Jesus leads, and you follow.

Imagine standing on the dance floor on your wedding day. It's the day you've dreamed of all your life, and you see the one you will spend the rest of your life with walking toward you. As he comes closer, he extends his hand and looks into your eyes. You can see his love for you mirrored in his gaze! Can you imagine how he feels knowing he has found the love of his life? He takes your hand and leads you onto the dance floor. His heart is full, no doubt, and so is yours. It's a dream come true! The same goes for Jesus. He is inviting you to join Him in the dance of your life—a dance into the new life He has for you.

The Father not only created us, but He also sent His only Son to die for us. More than two thousand years ago, on an old, rugged tree, Jesus was crucified and gave His life so that we could be cleansed of sin and live victoriously. He knew what was going to happen that day in the garden. Jesus understood from the beginning that He came to redeem mankind and restore their life. Know that you can have a life free of shame and rejection, with no more guilt – only freedom. Jesus knew a sacrifice had to be made, and He was willing to make that sacrifice for you and me.

Let's fast forward to a moment in your life when Jesus is the bridegroom coming to you, extending His hand. Surrendering to Him is like a dance where you let go and allow God to have His way. The word surrender has carried a negative connotation for a long time. We are afraid to surrender to what we don't know. We are so accustomed to living out our own plans that we can't imagine letting go and allowing Jesus to take the wheel.

That kind of surrender requires faith, and perhaps today your faith is in short supply. I realized after taking His hand that there is safety in surrender. I know Jesus has my best interests at heart. He came to set the captives free, and He wants you to be free as well. Free from anything that holds you down. Lastly, you will also experience power, love, and grace in surrender. Just as when you started learning to dance, you will face failures and may not always be perfect. There will be moments when you stumble in your walk with Jesus, but never forget that His grace, love, and power are always there for you. Jesus loves you!

Can you imagine how Jesus' heart must feel if someone says no to His invitation? "No, I am not interested in dancing, I will join the dance later, but I am not ready right now." It happens every day over and over, and I'm certain it breaks the heart of Jesus every time. He knows what is best for us. But we continue to think we know better.

The book of Hosea in the Old Testament speaks of the love our Father has for us. In Chapter 2, the story focuses on the people of God and how they had completely forgotten the Lord, pursuing their own desires instead. The people of Israel were following their own paths, but God loved them and continued to pursue them regardless. His love for us is immeasurable, and

He never gives up on us. In Chapter 2:14, God spoke through Hosea, saying, "I am now going to allure her, I will lead her into the desert and speak tenderly to her." He shares this with Hosea, confiding about Israel, His people. Out of love for them, God guides them into a desert experience for their own benefit. In those places, He can speak to them and reach them. A desert experience is where we often find ourselves alone and in a struggle. This experience is personal and varies for everyone. One thing is certain: when we find ourselves in that desert place, we want to be holding His hand, and we do not want to be so far away that we cannot hear God's voice.

Everyone will face a desert experience at some point in their lives. The desert is a place of correction and communication, where God can speak to His people. He led Israel into the desert and spoke tenderly as He walked beside them.

This lesson in God's love was the inspiration for the second verse of "Dancing with Jesus." "Is this the way it's supposed to feel? Dancing with Jesus, can it be real? I'm not afraid to go out into the deep, throw my arms around Him, and let Him lead."

The words to that song go right along with Hosea's message to us. God will speak tenderly to her. I can find confidence in this story. Knowing that as I step into the deep water, I am not alone; I am with Jesus. He will speak tenderly to me, and He will speak with you in the desert you are crossing. Your circumstances may be difficult, but rest assured, He will speak tenderly to you. If you are willing to take Jesus' hand and let Him lead, this dance can change your life. Do not be afraid of the deep; He is with you. Romans 8:28 promises, "All things work together for our good to those who love God and are called according to His purpose." The beauty of imagining dancing with Him allows us to shift our focus from our circumstances and pain to Him; we can see how He makes all things work for our greater good. So, print that scripture and place it somewhere you can see and read it every day.

Participation is the most beautiful aspect of viewing your relationship with Jesus as a dance. I don't know about you, but I don't want to miss out on anything that Jesus has planned for my life. I refuse to be the person sitting on the sidelines while others take a leap of faith. I want to live the life I was meant to live!

What about you? Are you even aware of what your walk with Jesus has in store for you? It is filled with great plans – plans to prosper you and not to harm you, to give you hope and a beautiful future.[2]

We were created for a "love" like this. I have decided not to settle and encourage you to adopt that same mindset. Speaking from experience, I can tell you that nothing will satisfy you like surrender, and nothing moves Jesus like your surrender. Jesus gave all on Calvary, and He simply asks for the same in return. I encourage you to accept His hand; say yes to the invitation. Lay down everything and allow nothing to stand between you and Jesus. Our heart is a throne room where something or someone sits; let it be Jesus, our Lord and Savior. Paul speaks about it in Hebrews Chapter 12:1, "Therefore, since we are surrounded by such a great cloud of witnesses, let us throw off everything that hinders and the sin that so easily entangles. And let us run with perseverance the race marked out for us."

It's not always going to be easy, but sometimes when you are walking on your journey, there is beauty that will find you; it is hidden around every bend in the road. The book of Isaiah talks about passing through deep waters and shares about times when we walk through the fire. Isaiah makes it clear that our pilgrimage can be challenging at times, but you will see the promise as you go. "I will be with you," says the Lord. "The waters will not sweep over you and when you walk through the fire, you will not be burned."[3] So you see, it's not a matter of if, but when, life carries us down roads we never imagined. It is then that I want you to see that Christ is stepping in and asking you to join the dance. Change your perspective! Adjust your lens and see that if or when you fail, you are falling into the arms of the Savior. Falling into Jesus' arms means you are on the dance floor. Trust, laugh, and weep while you dance. But whatever you do, dance!

I heard a song a few days ago that came at just the right time for me. Jesus is just like that; right when you think it's dark, He sends encouragement. The song I heard was written for a woman who had suffered greatly in her life, and the title is "Walking Through Fire." The chorus says, "Don't be afraid, I have redeemed you, I call you by name, beloved I see you."[4] If you can keep that thought at the forefront of your mind, knowing that Jesus sees you, nothing can steal your joy! It will be a beautiful day when you can trust like that. That is the secret to having the courage to join the dance.

Psalm 91:1-2 says, "He that dwelleth in the secret place of the most high shall abide under the shadow of the Almighty. I will say of the Lord, He is my refuge and my fortress: My God, in him will I trust." When this scripture begins to resonate deeply within you, nothing can stop you. Worry, anxiety, fear, and guilt will have no place to dwell when you choose to believe. You WILL abide under the shadow of the Almighty!

I will conclude this chapter with a little chorus that God gave me a few years back.

"Have I told you about my secret, that I live under Daddy's Smile, circumstances or difficulties can even stay a while. I'm a daughter of the King and He's the Son of righteousness, and until the Word melts away or I no longer want to stay, I will live all the while, underneath my Daddy's smile."

I want you to consider these words. They reflect your place with God. If we believe we have strayed from beneath those everlasting arms, then we need to stop, reflect, and remember.

God loves you, my friend. During the dance, you will discover that Jesus is faithful, and you will see His work every step of the way. Go ahead, put on some music and dance all over your kitchen and throughout your life with Him. It is a new day!

Cinderella's Castle

In January 2019, it was nearly time for me to make my travel arrangements to Orlando, Florida, for my training with The Airline Academy. Becoming a flight attendant had been a dream of mine since I was a senior in high school. God often presents opportunities in unexpected seasons of our lives. I remember hearing a successful businessman speak at a local church service. One statement in particular caught my attention. At the end of his speech, someone asked him to share one last word of wisdom—something that had helped him in his life and that he now strives to live by. Without hesitation, he answered, "Never miss an opportunity." Well, I had an opportunity in front of me, and I had a decision to make.

When I was a senior in high school, my dad won a trip to Hawaii for the whole family. He had a successful swimming pool business and built so many pools that year that he won this amazing trip. We were all very excited; we didn't often take trips as a family, so this was a real treat. My brother and I were especially thrilled because it was our first time flying. Departure day finally came, and when we arrived at the airport and checked in, the airport experience alone was fascinating. Then we saw this huge plane pull up to the terminal, and we could hardly believe what was happening. Since this was my first flight, as boarding began, my thoughts immediately turned to how this huge plane and all these people were going to get off the ground. My brother and I were taking it all in, peering out the window to watch the ground crew prepare for take-off. Once we were seated, the pilot announced that we would be taking off soon. Everything went smoothly; my brother and I were beside ourselves.

Soon, the flight attendants were up and serving refreshments. Back then, we called them stewardesses. Right away, I noticed their warm, friendly smiles and how they wanted to take care of us; we were their guests. As I watched them, I began to think about their responsibilities. My wheels were turning! First of all, they are getting paid to be kind to others and make us comfortable while flying the friendly skies. Second, they are on their way to Hawaii!

I started putting two and two together, and suddenly, I am solving another life dilemma of my youth: what to do after I graduate from high school. I struggled throughout high school; my concentration was off the charts, and my grades were nothing to brag about. I loved horses and enjoyed training them. I would have loved to be a horse jockey, but back then, there were no women jockeys; it was all men. I also considered the idea of being a fashion model, but I wasn't tall enough. I know these are significantly different paths – a jockey and a fashion model. I was that complex!

After further consideration of this new career choice – getting paid to fly, traveling the world, and having the opportunity to help someone – I may be onto something. After all, comforting a child or lending a hand to help someone is something I'd like to do for the rest of my life. I could get excited about that! After returning home, life moved on, and I didn't follow through with the plan to pursue a career as an airline attendant. If I could give you one piece of advice, looking back on that time in my life, it would be to pay attention to what you love and what you are passionate about; do what makes you come alive, because that's what the world needs: people who are alive and enjoying their journey!

I spent my life caring for my husband and the four amazing boys I was blessed with. I was a stay-at-home mom and loved every minute of looking after them. Oh, I cherished being their mother, their friend, and, since they were boys, their referee when needed. I also homeschooled them for most of their lives. We spent a lot of time together, and it was wonderful for me. Family was very important to me. It was hard work; I poured my heart and soul into training them to be the best boys they could be and to love God. I enjoyed teaching them about God and the love He had for each of them. I believed that if I could introduce them to a relationship with God at an early age, when they encounter difficult seasons in their own lives, they would know where to turn. As a mother, we want always to be there, but God loves them more than we do; He is the one who will always be there. After each one flew away like a little bird to pursue their dreams or marry their sweetheart, I found myself in a new chapter of life.

After 27 years of marriage, I was staring at a divorce. I have always said, "suddenly" comes into everyone's life. Through my own life experiences, I have learned that storms that have been brewing for too long can and will hit hard. During this time of difficulty, I began to experience those same feelings I had when I was a young high school student. What am I going to do? Who am I? What am I going to do with the rest of my life? Talk about things coming full circle.

This time would be different; I had the questions, but now I knew who to take them to. I had a strong relationship with God, and I knew He would help me answer those questions in time. Night after night, I spent a lot of time on the couch in prayer and meditation, seeking answers. One evening, God took me back to those days when I was about to graduate from school. Yes, He did! Have you been there? If you've lived long enough, then your answer is yes, no doubt! Take comfort, though; when this happens, God is up to something! Remember, with Him, nothing is wasted! That night, God reached down into the files of my life, pulled up the year 1982, and placed it in my lap. His timing is always perfect, and it was spot on; the exact direction I needed. I needed a purpose that would take the pain of loss away.

My heart and soul were my family, and my heart was broken. We are not prepared for the storms that enter our lives, but God knew all about it. After much prayer and wrestling with these questions, I decided to follow through on what God pulled from my past and placed in my future that night.

After 30 years, I was finally looking into The Airline Academy in Florida. They not only train you but also help with applying for a job within the airline industry. First, you receive training on the dos and don'ts of applying for a flight attendant position. It's not an easy industry to enter; the time invested in training would be beneficial. This was especially important for me since I had not been in the workforce for a long time. I asked the airline recruiter every question I could think of and got to know her well. I made phone calls daily for a while until I gathered enough information to make a decision. Weeks went by, and I still hadn't decided; it was a tough choice to make. Making decisions has never come easily to me; I was so afraid of making the wrong choice. Fear does that to us! Sometimes we have to step up to the plate and be brave. So, I did just that! I also felt that I needed an adventure.

I knew deep down this was the right decision because it was what I saw in front of me. Usually, when we pray about something, what appears before us is a good indication of our next step. So, I signed up! I'm going to airline school! It was a moment I found hard to process. In the days that followed, I felt like I was walking around in disbelief, but only for a short time, because there was work to do now. Online assignments were given to us before our arrival, and we needed to be prepared to take an exam on the first day. If you failed that exam, you would be sent home. This was just a glimpse of what the industry would be like: early mornings, tests, and daily exams—some announced and some not. It was just the beginning of this journey. Over the next few months, my life will be all about studying. Companies were hiring, and training with The Airline Academy would benefit me. Recruiters were seeking individuals interested in this profession. Graduating from the academy, learning about the industry, understanding emergency procedures, and consistently arriving on time every day would look great on my resume. It was worth the sacrifice for me to be there. We had reason to believe we might receive good news before leaving Florida. The opportunity to interview sounded exciting!

The online training was completed, and the day was approaching for me to fly to Florida for the remainder of my training. I was both excited and scared at the same time. Imagine me, a stay-at-home mom for over twenty years, now pursuing a career in the sky. Trust me when I say I was scared; looking back now, I see that God was with me. My family was there for me, cheering me on. God did what He does best: He carried me on.

I packed everything I needed and then some more. I would be gone for a week, but it felt more like a month. I said all my goodbyes to my kids and grandchildren; at that moment, I don't think I really understood what was truly happening. I continued to pinch myself day by day, because this was an adventure I never thought would come back to me at this time in my life.

Oh, what a wonderful Father who doesn't waste anything and remembers everything about you.

This was such a huge step for me, and since I hadn't visited Florida in a long time, I decided to leave early and spend a day at a Disney Park. You must understand something about me: I am a kid at heart. I wanted to take on this challenging endeavor, the airline academy, but I also thought I would have a little fun along the way. Something enjoyable can always help you get through the scary parts. Magic Kingdom was the park I chose to visit. It was a cloudy day when I arrived in Orlando, and I was concerned that the rain would spoil my plans for fun. I prayed and prayed, asking my Father to let me get there and to please stop the rain. I was so excited about that day at the park. You see, there was a reason I picked Magic Kingdom. There was someone I wanted to meet. After the plane landed, I jumped in an Uber, dropped off my luggage, and, smiling from ear to ear, I was on my way!

People were friendly in Florida, and I appreciated it; they had no idea who they were meeting. I was a small-town country girl, feeling like Cinderella before her prince found her. I was on a great adventure, shaking in my boots. As I arrived at this grand place, I was amazed to see highways and road signs welcoming me to this city. It felt like a whole different world. Another thing that always amazes me is the faithfulness of my Father and how He loves to answer our prayers. The clouds began to part, and the sun shone into the backseat of my car window as I was about to step out into one of the best days of my life – a day filled with surprises and a dance I will never forget!

I arrived! I was excited and anxious to get my ticket into the park. I wanted to spend as much time as possible in this beautiful place, and I wanted to meet Cinderella. Yes, I wanted to come to Florida a day early to meet Cinderella! I felt like a Cinderella girl myself. Cinderella had such childlike faith, and she trusted everyone. I know she is a fairytale character, but the little girl in me loves her. I was thrilled that this was happening to me. As I handed my ticket to enter the park, I was finally here, and I was blown away. I can't find the perfect words to describe what I was experiencing as I saw this place. I looked down the streets of this make-believe city, music was playing, and I was in complete amazement. I turned a corner and saw this beautiful castle in the distance. God not only held back the rain, but He also painted a beautiful sky as a backdrop. It made this moment unforgettable! I can close my eyes and see it even now.

I thought I was watching a movie on a giant screen, but it was all real. I walked up to this castle and reached out to place my hand on the wall. Tears filled my eyes as I stood there; I knew God was with me. Oh, where a dance with Him can take you, I thought to myself. Can this be real? Dreams do come true. God has provided it all because there is a plan. I took a picture of this moment, but even better, the image is painted on the walls of my heart forever. The day He brought me to the castle!

It reminds me of the experience I had the first time I saw the ocean. When I was young, we didn't go to the beach due to a tragedy in my family years ago, so I didn't see the ocean until I was around 12. My Sunday school teacher took her class to her beach house for the weekend. It was truly a priceless moment. I felt a similar sensation as we all walked toward the ocean. My first thought was, "What is this?" It's so vast that I can't wrap my mind around such a large body of water. It looked like a foreign land in the distance. I stood still, taking it all in. The only thing I could think to say was, "Wow!" The other girls were so excited that they didn't even hear me, and I'm glad they didn't, because they wouldn't have known what to think if they realized this was my first time seeing the ocean. My first visit to the ocean and my experience standing in front of Cinderella's castle created such an impactful moment for me—special moments that will never fade away.

So, after I picked my chin off the spotless paved streets of Magic Kingdom, I knew I needed to stay as long as possible that night. My family back home had told me that the park would stay open later on certain evenings, and this was one of those nights. You can purchase an after-hours ticket and remain in the park after it closes to the general public. It usually closes at 8 pm, but with my ticket, I could stay until 11:00 pm. I headed straight to the welcome center to buy my ticket; time was ticking, and it was getting closer to five o'clock. I walked in to purchase my extra ticket, feeling excited and sharing how this was my first time, since being a young girl, to see this magnificent place. I was sure my face gave it all away. There was a line, and as I waited, I started to feel fidgety. I could hear a parade passing by outside, and I was missing it. I was torn about what to do! Should I enjoy the park while it was still daylight or wait patiently to get the ticket and stay longer? I was faced with a difficult decision. I wish I could say I waited patiently, but I was anxious. After a few minutes, which felt like an hour, a sweet young girl came over to me, dressed in her adorable Disney outfit, and said, "Ms. Wood, we are so sorry that this has taken a few minutes of your time, but we would like to offer you a complimentary evening on us for the rest of your visit at Magic Kingdom." My eyes welled up with tears as I stood there; I find myself tearing up now while writing about the experience. I remember it so well. They had no idea about the turmoil my life had faced in the last few years, and they had no idea that God was using them and this experience for my healing. I smiled and would have loved to jump over the counter to hug them all, but since I couldn't, I gave them a big smile, accepted this blessing, and waved to them as I walked out the door.

When I stepped outside and onto the pavement of that street, I felt the arms of Jesus around me. Yes, that is the beauty of the dance; you have these moments where you feel His arms around you. This dance was here, and the music was playing everywhere; the time had come, and I had all evening. I am going to dance with Jesus in Magic Kingdom.

The evening progressed, and excitement filled every corner. It truly is a magical place. Cinderella's castle was beautiful! Just as the Cinderella movie depicts, she gave me the hope I needed. It is still my favorite movie, a perfect example of beauty for ashes and joy for mourning.

Well, my night continued as I explored the park, enjoyed the cutest rides, and visited the gift shops. Just walking down the streets was fascinating; music filled the air, not just any music, but beautiful Disney soundtracks from all the Disney movies. I recalled some of the rides from when I was a little girl; it was all coming back to me. A faint memory stored away in my young mind that God knew all about. Remember, nothing is wasted.

As the evening progressed, I began searching for a place to eat. My day started early, so I was feeling fatigued. I treated myself to a little snack and continued my journey through the park; I only had this one evening, so I wanted to fill it with as much as possible. My journey led me past a magnificent restaurant called Be Our Guest. It was a place my family recommended, and they even tried to get me reservations, but to no avail. Reservations for Be Our Guest must be made six months in advance. I was thrilled to see the place. "Beauty and the Beast" is another favorite movie of mine, and the restaurant's exterior looked just like it did in the movie.[1] A line of people waited outside, all eager to go in. A young lady was checking everyone in and verifying those who had reservations. That's when the wheels began to turn in my fairy tale head and childlike heart. I whispered a prayer. You guessed it! I asked Him to make a way for me to experience a night in this restaurant. You're probably as surprised as my family was when I tell you that God answered that prayer, and I found myself seated at one of the finest tables in the Grand Ballroom. I enjoyed dinner for two in the room where the characters from "Beauty and the Beast" danced in the movie. That's right, a table for two. My dance partner and I, whom no one else could see, sat in that ballroom, and I shared dinner with Him. I knew He was there. I never would have imagined in a million years that I would be here, but I was. I experienced the most exquisite food a Cinderella girl could ever have. Overjoyed, I pulled out my phone and shared the news with my family. I couldn't wait to tell them, and they were thrilled for me. It was truly an unforgettable evening.

I peeked into each room of the castle. Significant scenes from the movie "Beauty and the Beast" filled every space. Naturally, my favorite room was the ballroom. As I wandered around that room, I thought to myself, "Wow, I am strolling with Jesus in this ballroom, just as Belle danced with the Beast in the ballroom." What a breathtaking moment! I met the Beast that night; yes, the one I had seen in the movie all these years. The tall, hairy Beast depicted in the film was kind and a true gentleman, and I thanked him for the evening I spent in his castle. Well, I hesitantly turned and walked through the enormous wooden doors to exit this palace. Some exits are easy, but this one was hard to take; I didn't want this evening to end.

As I exited, the first thing I noticed was the dark sky and the lights in the park. It was night now, and the lights illuminated the sky, but not with stars—rather, with the most beautiful fireworks display I had ever seen. Just a few minutes later, I would have missed it. The timing was perfect! I had just stepped out of the restaurant onto the cobblestone street and was over-whelmed by this stunning sight in the sky.

It was no coincidence; my eyes filled with tears, and my heart was deeply touched by this moment that God allowed to happen for me. He was pouring out His love on me, and I truly believe He was showing me a glimpse of my future if I would trust Him. As I stood there gazing into the heavens, I thought of my mom and her sacrificial love for me. I wondered if she could see me; I hoped she could. I loved her so much. I thought of my dad, and I hoped he was standing next to Mom. I loved them. Their deaths were both so tragic, and seeing me standing in such a beautiful place, I knew it would bring a smile to them. I thought of my sons and their little families and how each one meant so much to me. I felt so blessed to be a mother, a grandmother, and a friend to each of them. I loved them all so much. I thought of my Heavenly Father, who loved me so much and how He carried me and my family through so much pain and sadness. There is nothing so tragic that He can't carry you through to the other side. I promise you.

Cinderella had to endure a lot; life was not easy or fair for her. Her positive outlook was beautiful and made all the difference. Even though it is a fairy tale, our stories are not! Life isn't fair or easy; it can be downright painful sometimes, but how you react is what truly matters. How you persevere and trust God with all your heart will make the difference. Look for the Prince of Peace! He will come. When you can lift yourself up and worship even when circumstances are not in your favor, God notices!

God will rescue you! He wants to bring you through; He desires to take you to the other side. He will do His part as long as you do yours. Be courageous! Move forward, even if you're afraid; go forward. This is what God wants for you: surrender and trust Him with your life.

More than two thousand years ago, Jesus walked the path that led to Golgotha and sacrificed His life for me and you.[2] It is not only the mountaintop experiences that highlight knowing Him as our Savior, but also the moment-by-moment conversations we can have with Him day by day. He wants you to know that on the hard days, you can lean on Him. So, will you let Him take you to the places He knows you would love to go? Will you trust Him in the dark times? Can you trust Him until the light comes? The light does come; it shines on your path and illuminates your heart in ways you can't imagine. Healing will come. You will see things you've never seen before. Your eyes will be opened, and when this happens, you will see so much clearer. It's like putting on glasses for the first time when you've had trouble with your vision. Yes, we can go around squinting, trying to make things out, but why would we? Put on the glasses!

Oh, friend, I hope you start looking with fresh eyes. The fireworks display in the sky that night, overlooking that magnificent castle, would not have been the same if it had been a little blurry. I know God orchestrated the whole evening for me because He loved me. I was a Cinderella girl, so He took me to the castle. Where will He take you? It's an adventure, this dance that I am describing to you. It is where your wildest dreams can come true!

As this lovely day came to an end, I finally met Cinderella. You remember I just needed to see her before I could leave the park. As I was on my way out, I passed the castle and noticed Cinderella's light was on in her room. Earlier that day, someone pointed out that this is where all the Disney princesses reside, and Cinderella was there now. Meeting her wasn't a coincidence; our footsteps are ordered. God wanted me to see that she wasn't dressed in an old, torn gown, her hair wasn't messy, and her face wasn't downcast. No, this is Cinderella after her prince had come. She's beautiful, her skin glows, and she radiates joy and peace. Her voice is like an angel's. Her dress glistens with all the colors of blue you can imagine. Her golden hair is perfectly done, and she wears a beautiful, shining tiara. This was the Cinderella I needed to meet. This was the image God wanted me to carry in my heart. God wanted me to realize something: no torn gown for His Cinderella; no downcast face, only joy and peace. I have a tiara that sits by my bed at home as a reminder that I am a daughter of the King. There's more I could tell you, but for now, I want you to remember something important. Cinderella never gave up, did she? She sat at her window, always humming a song. Her faith kept her going! Her fairy godmother spoke to her in the movie with these words. "If you lost all your faith, I couldn't be here, and here I am! You can't go to the ball looking like that; we have to hurry because even miracles take a little time."[3]

Don't stop believing in miracles! You could be on the brink of one!

The next morning came early; I hopped out of bed and prepared for my adventure to continue through the week. I passed that exam and was not sent home. The airline industry follows a principle: if you are on time, you are already five minutes late. That week, this was the golden rule. I made a point to arrive five minutes early.

During the training, I made many new friends. By the end of that week, I had an interview with a recruiter! Several were hired. I was offered a flight attendant trainee position with a great company based in Indianapolis, Indiana. In a few months, I will be leaving again for another month of training. This adventure was so beneficial for me and prepared me for what was to come, you know, baby steps. I was still scared, but I was also very excited about the wonderful experiences I encountered over the week. I couldn't wait to get home and share all the remarkable accomplishments that God allowed and supported me through during this trip.

Taking a new opportunity can be intimidating, but the confidence I gained in those seven days was priceless. I learned that you can do anything you set your mind to, and I was so glad that I followed through with God's plans that week. It's a dance; I show up, and Jesus shows up. He is faithful!! Romans 8:28 tells us that "All things work together for good to those who love God and are called according to His purpose." I carry Cinderella's story close to my heart; I remember how she lived.

She lived by faith, always had a song, and knew her prince would come. It's a fairy tale, and it's a great one!

Back to the Garden

I live in a beautiful country landscape in North Carolina. This morning, I am writing while sitting in my sunroom with the windows open. I can hear the sounds of nature all around me: owls hooting, leaves rustling, birds singing their unique melodies, the neigh of a horse, the snort of a deer, and waking up early to the crow of a rooster—likely very common sounds for Adam and Eve in the Garden of Eden. There's one thing I am certain of: the Garden of Eden wasn't a quiet place. Another thing I am sure of is that when the Father wants to speak to you, He will go to great lengths to get a word or an idea across to you. John 16:13 tells us this truth. "When the Spirit of truth comes, he will guide you into all truth; for he shall not speak of himself; but whatsoever he hears, he will speak and show you things to come."

I had a few months at home before leaving for flight attendant training. I wanted to use that time to paint my bedroom.

My vision was to transform my bedroom into a space reminiscent of the Garden of Eden. The Garden of Eden fascinated me as I read about the beautiful place God created for Adam and Eve to live. Imagine that! God wanted them to dwell in this magnificent garden. I believe He wants the same for us. I desired to live in that paradise, so I created a little Eden in my home. I love living things, so I envisioned vibrant trees and plants surrounding my bed as I awoke each morning. That would be an incredible way to start the day. Creating a space that would remind me daily, as I woke up, that God is right in the midst. Natural light streaming through the bamboo shades every morning. Tall green trees and foliage encircling my bed, and a cozy throw that would make me feel safe and warm as I slept. Soft gray and dusty pink were the colors I chose for this place of serenity. This transformation of my bedroom was inspired by a song called "Let It Happen" by United Pursuit. The part of the song that moved me the most was the bridge they sang repeatedly: "Take me back, back to the beginning, when I was young and running through the fields with You."[1] Again and again, I sang this melody, and the more I sang it, the more I envisioned this bedroom. Oh, Father! Take me back, back to the beginning! Yes! I wanted to inhabit that space I experienced even before I came to planet Earth.

Can you imagine life before you came here and think of yourself as a daughter of the King, running through the fields with Him? I am a country girl, so the fields are where I grew up, and I believe He knows just how to speak to us. God speaks to people in many ways because He understands how we, as individuals, hear and comprehend. As I sang and played this song, I started transforming this bedroom. It was exciting to see the change. After I finished the work, I stepped back and thought it was exactly as I had envisioned. There were trees and plants of all sizes with beautiful foliage, along with a grapevine I had made, adorned with little flowers that decorated my bed. Above my headboard, I wanted to find a picture of a little girl with long blonde hair running through a grassy field, looking as free as a butterfly. This was precisely the life I believed God truly wanted for me. He helped me see the vision and bring it to life. Most importantly, He wanted to take me back to the beginning. I am trying to help you understand that God is a personal, intimate friend.

Proverbs 29:18, "Where there is no vision, the people perish." If we pay closer attention to God's voice and our surroundings, we will see that He is all around us and speaking to us in many different ways.

A.W. Tozer shares this truth in his book, *The Pursuit of God:* "God is speaking always to us, but sometimes there is just too much noise, and it is hard to hear Him, and we miss moments when He is speaking to us. His words to us are the foundation of building a life of joy, peace, and knowledge of Him, and without it, we truly will perish."[2] I wish I could help you understand the importance of that statement. The Word of God is our foundation. We choose how we will live each day. Every morning that He wakes you up brings a new beginning. Adam and Eve walked and talked with God daily. We were created for fellowship, and He desires fellowship with you. In a relationship with a friend or our spouse, if we never communicate, we will never get to know that person. It is the same with God. Our relationship with Him grows through communication.

Matthew 22:14, "Many are called, few are chosen." Another translation reads, "Many are invited, few are chosen." I have always pondered this verse; I wasn't clear on its meaning until I walked there myself. We are all called to come to Jesus. Our response to that invitation makes all the difference in the world. Will you say yes? He is waiting for you! Will you let God have His way in your life, even when you don't see the plan? Will you have fellowship with the one who desires fellowship with you? John 10:27 says, "My sheep hear my voice, and I know them and they follow me." So, you must ask yourself: Are you hearing His voice, and are you obeying? If you are willing, He can use you to be a beacon of His light for others. People need hope, and He wants to use His chosen ones to shine that hope into the lives of others. Your life can be a testimony. We all have a story. Never let your story bring you down or make you feel like a victim, because God will use every part of it to help someone else who may have experienced exactly what you have. Nothing is wasted. He sent out the disciples, and He will send us out too; perhaps to a third-world country, neighborhood, marketplace, and most importantly, to our families.

When Jesus gave His life on Calvary for our sins, I want you to understand something about the reason. Jesus did not come and die on the cross out of sympathy for us; He came and gave His life because He was obedient to His Father. He knew what His obedience would bring when it was over. The resurrection could not happen without the crucifixion, the resurrection for Him and us! That was the beauty of it all: God was redeeming what happened in the Garden of Eden.

When we receive Christ and say yes, we become identified with Christ, His life, and death. We surrender our will for the Father's will, just as Jesus did. He prayed that night in the Garden of Gethsemane, "Let this cup pass over me; nevertheless, not my will, but yours be done."[3] That prayer, which is the Lord's Prayer, serves as a model for how we, as children of God, should pray. Our life is no longer our own; it is His life that we have surrendered to Him. In a way, this offers a form of liberation. It relieves us of the pressure to plan because we have entrusted our lives to Him. He has the plan. Matthew 7:11, "If you then, being evil, know how to give good gifts to your children, how much more will your Father who is in heaven give good things to those who ask him!" Our foundation starts right there. Building a strong foundation begins with the same prayer Jesus prayed to the Father. Our foundation is Christ. I am a visual learner, so I needed to create that space in the garden to truly grasp this wonder.

It may take some time as you seek the Lord, but I promise it will be the beginning of the good things He has stored up for you. Jeremiah 29:11, a verse that hangs in my bedroom, "I know the plans I have for you, declares the Lord. Plans to prosper you and not to harm you, to give you hope and a future." I have stood on this verse and love each word that Jeremiah was trying to convey. We need His Word to live each day, and sometimes, when days are hard, we need His Word for every moment.

One morning, as I sat on my bed, I opened my Bible to the book of Genesis. In those first few verses, I knew God wanted to show me something. "God created the heavens and the earth; darkness covered it, and the Spirit of God hovered over the waters."[4] So, we see that the darkness was there; He created it that way and hovered over it all. The first thing God said was, "Let there be light," and He separated the light from the darkness.[5] He didn't drive out the darkness; He made a distinct difference between the two. Know this: the darkness that was there was not darkness to Him. Psalm 139:12 says that darkness is not dark to you; the night is bright as the day, for darkness is as light with you. However, we are not God, and you and I do not always recognize the darkness sometimes hiding in our hearts. We need Him to help us and shine the light. Yes, even when we live daily in fellowship with Him, there is still darkness in our hearts, and we need Him to shine the light. His Word will shine if we are willing to look. We are in utter darkness until He shines His light. Darkness would have been upon the face of every man and woman if the Son of God had not come to the earth two thousand years later and brought light and life to us. The rest of the story is that Adam and Eve disobeyed in that garden and were cast out. However, God had a plan to bring about redemption to all mankind. He loved us while we were sinners. The world has an opportunity, an invitation, to come into this light. In the beginning, the Lord saw the light that day and said, "It is good."[6] How much greater when we see the light that He brings to us. That is a good day, too!

A beautiful love story beckons us to rise from the ashes and allow Him to bring beauty into our lives. II Corinthians 6:14, "What fellowship has light with darkness?" I believe He is trying to say those two will never be reconciled! No grey area there! Light and darkness are two distinct differences. On the very first day, God separated light from darkness. As we come to Him, He will also separate the darkness within us and bring forth light, which dispels darkness. Jeremiah 17:9, "Our hearts are deceitful above all things and desperately wicked; who can know it?" This verse describes our heart until God shines light into it!

Trusting Jesus on the dance floor means you trust Him with your life. For Jesus to reveal your heart, you need to be willing for Him to be Lord over your heart. So, the question is: do you want to go back to the garden? Are you willing to step out from behind the fig leaf and let Him gently expose anything that He sees that is not good for you? Psalm 23:3, "He restores my soul." He wants to restore everything to His sons and daughters to the original version if they are willing to follow Him. Don't settle; be the original!

I don't think I came up with the idea to transform my bedroom into a Garden of Eden; rather, I believe it was the Holy Spirit guiding me. It was an experience that God wanted me to go through so He could speak to me in ways He knew I would understand. It may not be a garden that He will use for you, but trust me, He knows how to speak to you. You are God's creation.

I want to go now to another garden, the Garden of Gethsemane. We know Jesus prayed in this garden. The night of His betrayal happened in this garden. Jesus and His disciples were there, and Jesus went to pray. He knew His time was upon Him.[7] The Bible says Jesus prayed to the Father and asked, "Oh My Father, if it be possible, may this cup pass from Me, nevertheless not as I will, but as You wilt."[8] What was the cup? It was a cup of suffering and death to atone for the sins of the world. It was God's will. The betrayal by one of His disciples, soldiers mocking Him, being spit upon, and receiving thirty-nine stripes were all part of what Jesus endured for us, carrying a heavy wooden cross up a hill to Golgotha, where He was crucified. Jesus suffered an agonizing, slow, and painful death for us. It was intended to be a public humiliation. He was made a spectacle, even though He could have called down angels to save Him. Our sins were laid upon Him so we could receive forgiveness and life, not only life here on earth but eternal life! Jesus came to the earth for this purpose. It was truly a sacrifice of love for all of mankind.

When you choose to accept Jesus, you receive forgiveness, and your identity is now in Christ. This means you have decided to let Christ enter your life and wash away your past sins. But that's not the only benefit; you also identify with Christ, which means you share in His death. When you identify with

Christ, you become a child of God. You give your life to God, surrendering your own plans so that His plan becomes your path. When He died, you died as well. You let go of your way of doing things and now bring every situation to Him. If you are wise, you will allow Him to counsel and guide you. It is a beautiful place of surrender.

We may walk through a valley; we may walk through fire, but we come through to the other side. He walks with us all the way. In Matthew 16:24, Jesus goes on to say to his disciples, "Whoever wants to be my disciple must deny themselves and take up their cross and follow me." Will you hang on to the self-life and keep your heart of stone, or will we give your heart to God? Trust Him with all the broken pieces? When you give up and let God have His way, you will understand what it means to be identified with Christ in His life and death.

The gospel, the "good news," is not Christ for me unless I decide to let Christ be formed in me. Let me say that again: it's not Christ for me, but Christ be formed in me! That is the good news!

I was at this place a few years ago and didn't realize my broken heart was crying out for its way. I wanted things my way. I understand the struggle; I had a broken heart and was still trying to fix it, but there comes a time when we need to drop the fig leaf and let things come to the surface. The struggle is real. We are hurting. I loved God, but I loved some other things, too. They were competing for my allegiance to God. Nothing or no one can take the place of God. He is to be our first love.

Matthew 16:24: "Whoever wants to be my disciple must deny themselves." Denying myself means I don't get to lead in the dance. Jesus invited me! Was I going to let Him lead? Do I want to be His disciple? Absolutely! I knew He was the only one who could restore me.

I encourage you to trust God because after the breaking, He can completely put your life back together. Although breaking can be painful, it's only when this hard outer shell of our self-life is shattered that He can fully come into our hearts. He reveals Himself to us, allowing us to become all we were created to be. Have you experienced a breaking of your independence? Do you understand what it means to be crucified with Christ? Do you realize that God's breaking will ultimately benefit you?

To truly understand, look at the cross and what came after the crucifixion. The resurrection came! It brought us salvation, but that's not all! Healing, deliverance, and freedom followed, too. All these promises and more are now ours because of Jesus' sacrifice at Calvary. Galatians 2:20, "I have been crucified with Christ; it is no longer I who live, but Christ lives in me." Psalms 103 lists our benefits in Christ. "He forgives our sins, heals our diseases, redeems our lives from the pit, and crowns us with love and compassion. He satisfies your desires with good things." Psalm 103:11 speaks of His Love, "His Great Love for those who fear Him." Our number one prayer should be to fear Him, both for ourselves and our loved ones. Proverbs 9:10 declares, "The fear of God is the beginning of wisdom, and knowledge of the Holy One is understanding."

Jesus told Mary, Lazarus's sister, that He was the resurrection and the life![9] He raised Lazarus from the dead, and that's just what He desires to do with your life. He wants to take the ashes, heal the broken heart, gather the scattered pieces of your life, and give you back a better life. Can you say hallelujah? I needed Him to do that for me, and He met me in the pit and pulled me out. That's why I share my testimony through the pages of this book! If He can do that for me, He can do that for you! Cry out to Him. Hebrews 5:7 says, "Jesus offered up prayers and petitions with fervent cries and tears to the one who could save him from death, and he was heard because of his reverent submission." You are heard when you cry out to God. I promise you!

I believe the struggle for some people is that they did not have a relationship with their earthly father while growing up. Maybe they had a dad, but he wasn't present in their lives. Therefore, their view of their heavenly Father is the same. They can't fathom God's unwavering love for them. I struggled with it, too. When I was a young girl, my dad was present but not part of my life. He wasn't the dad who sat me on his lap, held me in his arms, and let me know that I was his special little girl. I never knew what it was like to be daddy's little girl. When I became a teenager and had no relationship with Him, I couldn't understand why He wanted to intervene in my life then. Until that point, I felt completely unnoticed. I felt so invaluable. This can interrupt a young girl's life and set it on a path of utter destruction. Utter destruction doesn't always mean outwardly;

the internal destruction is real as well. Self-doubt and negative thoughts are equally as bad. Through many years of struggling, I now know God is a Father to the fatherless. That truth is manifested in Psalm 68:5: "He is a Father to the fatherless, a defender of widows is God in His Holy dwelling."

If you have felt abandoned and experienced rejection, I want to share something important with you. God was there with you through it all! You are here because God brought you here! You are reading this book because He guided you to it! You went through deep waters, but they did not overtake you because He held them back. You may have come through scathed, but you possess a sound mind, strength, and a God who loved you through it all. You are still here because His plan remains intact in your life. Let that sink in. Reflect on some moments from your childhood and see if you can identify His hand in those situations. Did He intervene in some way for your benefit? Can you recognize how He was present even though He didn't take you out of it, helping you to endure it?

Why is it hard to trust? It might be that due to all the hurt you have endured and the times you felt so alone, you didn't believe God was there. I understand; I felt that way too, but I have looked back over my life and can certainly see moments and places where He was indeed present. I was just overwhelmed by the voices shouting the opposite. Amid chaos and dysfunction, the Word reminds us that He is there. Choose to believe it. I have walked with Him, and I am convinced of His presence surrounding me. I hope this message helps you see that He is there for you, too. It may have been tough for you; it was tough for me as well, but it will not be wasted. God will use every bit of it! Jeremiah 33:3 proclaims, "Call to me and I will answer you and will tell you great and hidden things that you have not known."

I remember one day when I was really struggling. I picked up my guitar and began to play. God gave me these words. I believe it was a message from Heaven. The name of the song is "Scattered Pieces." When we experience brokenness and pain—maybe the loss of someone special or a marriage that you thought would last forever—then you know what I mean by "pieces." You have been so broken that you feel there are only pieces left of you. You don't even know how you could pick them up and move forward. I have been there, and I thank God He found me there and didn't leave me. He picked up the pieces gently, one at a time.

These are the words He gave me in that difficult place: *scattered pieces of a broken life. Some are lost, while others are just covered with strife. But I come to the Master, holding the pieces in my hand, and what He said in that moment, I hope you understand. He said, "Daughter, that's all I need, and to my Son, I can work with these. I just need you to trust in me, and some of you just believe that I can take your broken pieces and make a masterpiece."*

His words to me that day were a message that came from crying out to Him, and He is faithful to answer. I believe He can take broken pieces and turn them into a masterpiece. That is how faith works. God always confirms things in His Word.

A few days later, I was reading Genesis chapter 15. It contained the story of the covenant God made with Abram, promising that his offspring would be as numerous as the stars in the heavens, if they could even be counted. The challenge was that Abram was now an old man, and his wife, Sarai, was beyond the age of having children. Abram struggled, just as we do at times; yet God spoke, and Abram believed. However, being human, he asked God for a sign so he would know this promise would come to pass.[10] In verse 9, God gave him instructions on what to do: "Go, build an altar Abram, and get a sacrifice and take this sacrifice and cut it into pieces and lay them out on the altar." This request was consistent with what God had asked many times in the Old Testament—to build an altar and offer Him a sacrifice. This time, though, God specifically instructed him to cut the sacrifice into pieces. God was always specific about the altar and the sacrifice. Abram obeyed and did exactly as he was told, and as the sun began to set, he fell into a deep sleep, and it even mentions that thick, dreadful darkness came over him. Verse 17 continues, "A smoking firepot and blazing torch appeared and passed between the pieces." The pieces that Abram had cut up. Then I understood what He was showing me. I had nothing but pieces, and some of you have nothing but pieces left, but it is the pieces that He wants. If we give Him the pieces we have left of our lives, He accepts them as an offering to Him. The Lord made a covenant with Abram that

He would give him a child, descendants, and land to dwell in. God also understands that we are mere humans, so He provided Abram with a sign of His promise. Because of my faith, I believe that God knew I needed that verse that day and wants to reveal Himself to those with childlike faith.

"The god of this age has blinded the minds of the unbelievers so that they cannot see the light of the gospel that displays the glory of Christ, who is the Image of God."[11] The Word of God is powerful for those who believe, powerful enough for you and me to become sons and daughters of God. But it is all about believing! It doesn't matter where you are or what you have done; this is why Christ came: to save and to heal. Jesus' Words were just that: He didn't come to call the righteous, but sinners to repentance. The day I gave Him the pieces left from my brokenness and laid them out before Him, and began to worship Him, is the day the healing began.

No one can choose for you; you must make the choice. Will you become His bondservant and allow Him to have His way in your life? He has promises to fulfill for you. Remember again, Jeremiah 29:11: "I know the plans I have for you, declares the Lord. Plans to prosper you and not to harm you, to give you hope and a future." He is your Father, so His plans for you are good.

Are you struggling with doubt and unbelief? Stop right there! Acknowledge it and adjust your focus. It's that simple. Yes, just redirect your attention to Jesus, the author and finisher of your faith. Remember, He wants you to come just as you are, and know that nothing from your past is wasted. Jesus will redeem and restore every broken piece!

The Life of the Eagle

G od is so faithful! When you ask God to help you take the next step, He is always there. He is waiting for us to ask Him for help. If we could only understand how much He loves us and recognize that He is all around us, our lives could be incredibly peaceful, even amidst chaos. At times, it is hard to believe that God Almighty is pursuing me and wants to assist me with every difficult step. We often think God is far away, when all the while He is just waiting for us to notice Him.

Just the other day, I saw Him! I dropped by a consignment shop, looking for something specific. When I approached the area for the item I needed, I spotted a message that resonated deeply with my spirit printed on a shirt. It was a word that spoke to me straight from the mouth of God. The message on the t-shirt was "Be patient with your journey." As soon as I saw it, my heart settled down. We often get frustrated with ourselves; not only do we hold high expectations of others, but we also set high standards for ourselves. When frustration arises, we should pause and reflect on how far we've come on this journey called life. Some of us aren't very good at that, so God steps in and reminds us. "Be patient young lady, you've taken some big steps on your own." He did that for me that day in a local consignment shop.

As I was praying one morning, lying before Him and talking to Him, I felt I was in a place where I truly needed to seek help with this next step. I was feeling very uneasy; I knew it was another step of faith. So, I prayed and asked Jesus to help me. Soon after, I got up and went about my day. Looking back now, I realize He let me run into someone at the grocery store a week ago that I hadn't seen in years. We laughed and hugged; we were so glad to see each other, and I'm pretty sure we shed a tear together. God already knew I needed help, and He was lining it all up.

The visit with my friend at the grocery store resulted in a text from another friend we both knew, one I hadn't seen in years. She had also faced great disappointment in her life. One visit led to another, as that's what friends do for each other. We sat down for coffee together, and it was exactly what I needed. Sometimes, a visit with a friend or even a stranger who has walked the same road, been in the same valley, and come through can make all the difference. We need each other in life, and since our steps are ordained, God orchestrated both encounters for the encouragement I needed.

I was journaling recently, and after I filled the page with my thoughts and gratitude for the day, I turned the page. At the top of a new page was the scripture, Psalm 103:5: "He fills my life with good things so that I stay young and strong like an eagle." As I saw this scripture, I was reminded of the eagle. It was no coincidence. I immediately recalled a message I heard years ago about the "molting eagle." It was one of those messages you never forget. I have a book in my library titled "Life of the Eagle."[1] I went to retrieve it from the bookshelf. With anticipation, I opened the book; I knew God was speaking to me and wanted to reveal something to me. He allows a scripture to appear before us, or a book to be in the right place at the right time; sometimes it's a message on a t-shirt, and sometimes it's a still, small voice.

As I began to read this book, a scripture that I have read many times came to mind. Isaiah 40:31 says, "But they that wait upon the Lord shall renew their strength; they shall mount up with wings as eagles; they shall run and not be weary and they shall walk and not faint." Goodness! Renewing strength, running and not being weary, walking and not fainting are all the things we need, but what does the eagle have to do with them?

It was the molting eagle that God wanted me to remember, and what the eagle had to face in his life. This event occurs at the pinnacle of the eagle's life, around the age of 45 to 50. As the eagle begins to weaken, its feathers start to fall out, its talons become very brittle, and its beak begins to break down and crumble. It is a dying process that every eagle faces. It is called the molting eagle. He is in the fight of his life, and if he doesn't win the fight, he will die. This lengthy ordeal is something the eagle must endure, so he retreats to a remote place; it is the greatest test of an eagle's life. His strength and endurance will have to hold out until the very end. Feathers will fall out so they cannot fly, talons break down so they cannot walk, and their beak will break down, making eating very difficult. I could not believe what I was reading as I heard this story for the second time. Oh, the timing of God, sending the message we need to hear at the perfect moment in our struggle. The biblical verse becomes clearer to me as I read on, and the story improves as it develops into a beautiful love story.

Eagles mate for life, a remarkable act of dedication. During the molting period of an eagle's life, their mate helps sustain it. It is a sweet story, but there may be more profound truths about why God provides us with someone special to share our lives with. I am reminded of my own story. The eagle finds a high place to rest. Its mate plays a crucial role in saving its life. The faithful partner begins to drop food and continually flies back and forth over the eagle. Other eagles that have also gone through this process soar above and scream, making loud screeching sounds to encourage the eagle to fight for its life. Who knows what the eagle understands? It is incredible what we can learn by observing nature. It is up to the eagle to reach for the food and eat while enduring the pain. With no talons to grip, they must pull with what little strength is left to get close to the food. This part is painful for the eagle. The process continues as long as they remain alive. Slowly, as the eagle struggles to survive day after day, it begins to grow stronger. Its beak starts to grow, new feathers appear, and talons begin to develop. One can imagine the daily perseverance they must endure while waiting for their life to start anew. If the eagle survives this period in its life and wins the fight, this part is amazing! The eagle's lifespan will be doubled, allowing it to live another 50 years. So, the eagle waits, resting in its safe place, accepting the help it desperately needs, and fighting through to recovery.

After rereading this book, Psalm 103:5 has taken on a whole new meaning for me and hopefully for you, too. "He satisfies your desires with good things so that your youth is renewed like the eagle." Another encouraging verse, Isaiah 40:31: "But they who wait for the Lord shall renew their strength, they shall mount up with wings like eagles; they shall run and not be weary; they shall walk and not faint." Now we understand why they run and do not get weary. Once God has renewed your life, you will want to run too. You can run as fast as a Thoroughbred out of the gate because you have been transformed.

It's hard to wait, but hopefully, now you see that you have something to look forward to. I read something recently that I had never thought of before. God is patient, and of course, we know that He has every virtue. But think about the patience God had as He waited for Noah to build an ark to save his family from the flood. God had to do some serious waiting, and sometimes He asks us to do the same. He does want to fill our lives with good things, and sometimes we need to remember that He is working things out for our greater good, but we will have to wait. Just as the eagle lies out on that rock under the sun, waiting to spread its wings so it can soar back into the sky, that eagle will one day be the eagle helping others who are going through the molting process.

The sad truth is that some eagles don't make it through this process. As the eagle lies on the rock of a high cliff, it can see the leftover carcasses of those who didn't survive. The lesson is that the molting eagle had to participate in the help he was receiving; there had to be effort in taking the nourishment, understanding that he had to be still and wait for his strength to return. That is the reality of it all: even with God's help, we have to choose to participate in our own recovery.

Now, after learning about this amazing creature, ask yourself what takeaways you should have from this lesson. Why did God allow the eagle to double its life? I think God may also be considering us in this lesson. Why is there scripture about it, and why does He compare us to the eagle? I believe it is the waiting. I think that waiting is what God is trying to emphasize and its importance. We often view waiting as if God's answer is no, but that is not what He is saying. When we are waiting, God is working things out for us! Waiting is not "no." It is also not the time to look at your surroundings and think this is how things will always be. When you are waiting, you can trust that God is working. We try to get ahead of God; we think we need to assist Him, when clearly, He wants to lead us. I encourage you to let Him clarify things for you. Save yourself some heartache and don't attempt to help God. Don't make the mistake of seeking counsel from everyone except God. It's okay to seek advice from others, but the first and final say should come from our greatest counselor, God. Jeremiah 33:3: "Call unto me, and I will answer thee, and show thee great and mighty things, which thou knowest not." Never forget that verse!

When I need help or I'm feeling confused or struggling, I run to my favorite place in my home, lie down on the floor on my soft blanket, and have a conversation with Him. There is something about taking this position with Him on the floor. It's worth sharing for sure! I like to lie before Him because I desire to get as low as I can in the presence of a Mighty God. You can't get any lower than the floor, so I believe it's such a beautiful expression of surrender, letting Him see that I know He is above all things in my life, and He alone has the answers I need.

The 28th chapter of Matthew recounts the story of the visit to the tomb by the women who stood by Him throughout the crucifixion. Mary Magdalene and another woman named Mary visited the tomb on the third day, which was the day of the resurrection. Perhaps you know the story; the angel met these ladies and told them, "He has Risen, come and see the place where He lay. Go quickly and tell His disciples He has risen from the dead and you will find him in Galilee."[2] As they were leaving the tomb, afraid yet filled with joy, they met the Lord. When they came upon Jesus, they fell at His feet and worshipped Him. Yes, they must have known something about how to present themselves before the Lord Almighty.

I never regret stopping everything in the middle of my day so I can go before Him, casting my cares on Him. Sometimes I can't pause and take my position of surrender on the floor because of where I am at the time. But I still cry out a whisper to Him and ask for His help. He is Jesus, the lover of my soul. Just like the eagle, He wants to double my lifespan too. He desires to give us life and life more abundantly! That can only happen when we surrender to Jesus. What else can we do while we wait? We can worship. We can thank Him for the prayers He is going to answer. When you feel weary and discouraged, that is the best time to worship. It is faith in action! Just as the eagle waits on that rock high up on a cliff, he knows a transition is taking place. Worship until the weariness and discouragement dissipate, because they will. Yes, you are crying out from your heart; know that He hears your cry. Like Bartimaeus, a blind beggar, when he heard that Jesus was coming into town, he started crying out to Jesus. The crowd told him to be quiet, but Bartimaeus just yelled even louder.[3]

Another beautiful story is found in the Gospel of Mark, chapter 5. It tells of a woman who needed healing. She had suffered for twelve long years, spending all she had on physicians, but her condition only grew worse. When she heard Jesus was in town, she pressed into the crowd, just wanting to touch Him. She said, "If I may touch but his clothes, I shall be whole." Jesus felt that touch from her. He has bowels of compassion for us. He healed her and told her, "Your faith has made you well."[4] So let me encourage you to ask Him for whatever you need.

Jesus is the way, the truth, and the life. Surrender to the one who knows all about surrendering and hung on a cross out of obedience to His Father to redeem each of us. As I write this chapter, it just happens to be Easter weekend. In the spirit of the season, I watched the movie "The Passion," and my heart is still overwhelmed by what Jesus sacrificed for me on the cross. He paid the price, obeyed the Father, and He redeemed us. There is no greater love, an incomprehensible love.

The outcome will be marvelous for you, just like the story of the eagle. "They who wait for the Lord shall renew their strength; they shall mount up with wings like eagles; they shall run and not be weary; they shall walk and not faint."[5] The eagle spreads its wings and lifts itself off that rock to fly high in the sky; can you imagine how the eagle must feel? God wants you to know how the eagle feels! He wants you to experience the same redemption, another chance. He wishes you a joyful life today and in eternity, too.

It's Time

"It's time." I remember waking up early one morning in the spring of 2018 to those words. As I lay there with my head still on the pillow, staring at the ceiling, my immediate thought was, "It's time for what?" I was working at the florist that day, so I got up, dressed, and hit the road. But those words followed me throughout my day.

The truth is, it's not the first time, nor will it be the last time that I hear God's voice in the early morning. When I awaken to a song, I know that He has been singing over me as I slept. "I will praise the Lord who counsels me; even at night my heart instructs me."[1] While we sleep, God continues to minister to us. He created us in such a way that, if we let Him guide us, the sky is the limit. He speaks to us in many ways. He speaks when we are awake, and He speaks while we sleep. It could be a dream, a song, or just a still, small voice, but He speaks. Oh, what a good Father we have! There is nothing sweeter than hearing His voice, but this time it was different; it felt more like a proclamation. He was letting me know that something is coming. "My sheep hear my voice, and they know me and follow me."[2] When I receive a word, I write it down. When we hear from God, it is worth writing down. Mary, Jesus' mother, when told she would have a child, even though she was a virgin, pondered it in her heart and spoke of it to no one. She reflected on all that the angel of the Lord had spoken to her.[3]

After receiving the words, "It's time," so much has changed. I would like to tell you I didn't question God in all that has happened, but that would not be the truth. I trusted as best I could. I certainly needed His grace and assurance daily, and sometimes in the moment. Trusting is hard at times. I have learned, though, that in the questioning, if we wait, He makes it all clear.

"Sorrow is better than laughter because a sad face is good for the heart."[4] You might think the same thing I thought the first time I read this scripture: "Oh, this is why all this is happening to me – a sad face is good for the heart." The Lord spoke to me one day while I was praying those exact words back to Him. The reply was quite different from what I expected. He said, "This is not happening to you; this is happening for you." Well, ponder that! It will change your perspective. Just a few words from the Lord can change everything! Your perspective can shift, and that is often what we need in our situation. Shift out of neutral, out of reverse for sure, and shift into drive. Yes! Drive! Drive a little faster so you can build momentum and get out of that pit quicker.

I opened my Bible this morning to read Psalm 102. To be honest, I didn't want to read that one. I preferred to meditate on Psalm 139, one of my favorites, but I knew the Holy Spirit was leading me. So, I followed because I believe His ways are better than mine.

This Psalm He was leading me to is about an afflicted man lamenting before the Lord. As I began to read, I came to verse nine, and that is where He had my attention. It says, "For I eat ashes as my food and mingle my drink with tears because of your great wrath, for you have taken me up and thrown me aside." As I continued reading, verse 13 says, "You will arise and have compassion on Zion, for it is time to show favor to her, the appointed time has come." I was immediately reminded of that morning, just a few days ago, when I heard those words, "It's time."

God was showing me something! Your mind goes to the people and situations in your life when you are listening to the voice of God. However, in my experience, I have come to realize that when He speaks a word to me, it is most often for me. As I sat there reading that Psalm and meditating on it, I became overwhelmed by His love. I had felt a little worried about those words, "It's time." We become fearful when we hear or receive a word, but there was nothing to fear; God was saying something different. I was the afflicted man in the story. I was the one in distress, eating the ashes as my food and mingling my drink with tears. That was me, and it had been me for a long time. Oh, to have God's favor and compassion! I was ready to hear those words. I turned to that Psalm daily and read it so often that my Bible would flip to it automatically. When God gives you a scripture, hold on to it! Don't let it out of your sight! Memorize it!

Loneliness can creep in, and I sometimes felt alone because my mother and father were no longer here with me, and my marriage of over twenty-five years had ended. When devastating things happen, you can feel overwhelmed, and nothing compares to the Father's timely words, which comfort you and remind you that He sees you in that place. He reassures us that we are not alone. When such times arrive, we think our lives are over and that we know how the future will unfold, but God sees something entirely different. He sees the person He created and knew long before we were born. He knows the purpose for which you were created and the beautiful plan He has for you.

Yesterday, as I drove down the street in my neighborhood, simply observing the houses and the families that each home represented, I was acutely aware that my house resembled the aftermath of a cruel storm. I asked Jesus this question, "What is it you want to do for me now that you couldn't do for me before?" Have you ever pondered that question? You see, friend, sadly, I have been in this broken place before. I know how it feels to be left and abandoned; I understand the crippling nature of rejection and how it seeks to destroy you. I recognize how difficult it is to gather the scattered pieces of your heart. I know what it's like to try to regain your footing. This was now the second time I had to piece together a shattered heart and carry on. My marriage was ending, and my heart was broken.

As I ate the ashes and mingled them with my tears daily, I reflected on all the heartache I had endured. I reflected on my childhood and realized that the environment didn't help me at all. My dad was a great provider, but he wasn't the father who could or would nurture his children. He seemed to believe that our mother was responsible for that, while he focused on working and providing us with a safe place to live. He was indeed a good provider, and I'm not disputing that, but a dad's role in the family is so important. If they are absent, well, you feel it. Our mother was one amazing woman and the best mom any child could ask for, but she couldn't fill the role of dad. His decisions and his lack of involvement were still harmful. As I grew older, I came to understand that my dad was also hurting from his childhood trauma. He couldn't show us the love we needed from him. Either he was filled with anger and pain from wounds he couldn't express, or he wouldn't love us in the way a child requires. Ultimately, the truth is, we get to choose. God has given us the beautiful privilege of free will. The truth is, we can change all the negativity passed down from previous generations. We have the power to draw the line, put a stake in the ground, and say, this stops here!

For years, I hoped and prayed my dad would find healing and comfort from God because he was held captive in a pit. Sadly, the pit that gripped him destroyed him. My brother and I loved him with all our hearts, and our families suffered and were wounded by his choices. It is God's grace and hand in each of our lives that we are here today in a better place. It is all because of Jesus! This doesn't mean tribulations don't come, but we begin to see through the lens of God. In this view, there is hope, and where there is hope, there is life. We are here on this earth because He wanted us here. Our fathers and mothers brought us here, but we were thought about and planned long before we arrived. When we arrive on this earth, we are given choices, and those choices make all the difference. Through God's plan of redemption, Jesus invites us to come to Him and bring all our sins, and not just our sins, but the wounds we have carried as well. In this life, we will get hurt, but Jesus wants to heal us. He wants to bring us salvation and lead us to a life of freedom so we can live our best life.

As a little girl, I grew up feeling alone. I was a country girl who loved her horse. After school and chores, I headed straight for the barn. I was often alone, and I now realize how the enemy manipulated me into believing lies that were not true. It may have looked on the outside that I was alone, but I have now come to see that I was never alone. The truth is that what you pick up when you are young, truth or lie, will be the lens you look through until it is corrected. Throughout my childhood, I spent a lot of time thinking and processing the things I was struggling with. Looking back, I realize I could have benefited from professional help with the processing. As I grew into an adult with no one to discuss these things with, I believed the lies the enemy had planted. Half-truths that he twisted. Since my dad didn't show me love, I believed he didn't love me. I embraced that lie. I also believed I wasn't special or of any value. I must not be pretty enough, or Daddy would have felt different towards me. Shame and self loathing drove their cruel claws into me, and I formed those awful, deep-rooted opinions of myself in my heart.

It happens slowly to you, and you don't even realize it. Remember the "Giants in the Land" speech at my brother's graduation ceremony? It was a giant that had a grip on me, and it stemmed back to this little girl who wanted her dad. I wanted to hear him say all the things a little girl wants to hear. I wanted to know he cherished me. I wanted to sit on his lap, just like I saw all my other friends sitting in their dads' laps. I just wanted to feel special. I wanted to feel safe. What happens instead is you feel like you're the problem. The questions the enemy plants in your little heart are, "What is wrong with me? How could a dad not pay attention to his little girl?" So, this is where the enemy did his deceptive work, entangling me and trying his best to destroy me.

Like in the Garden of Eden with Eve. The enemy came to her with a question. "Did God say you would die if you ate of that tree?" He began with Eve by planting a seed of doubt in her mind, and it worked.[5] He continues to work in this manner with people every day, even now. We live our lives doubting, don't we? We doubt we are enough, we doubt we are pretty, and we doubt we can achieve our dreams. The thought was planted, and Eve started to doubt. She responded with her own question, "Maybe I didn't hear God?" For me, it was, "Maybe I am not special?" We both bought it, hook, line, and sinker. The enemy will use truth and twist it to bring confusion into your mind. No wonder the name Satan means twister, because that is what he does best. He twists the truth into lies that we start believing. The truth is, God was there all along. His Presence was with me through all of the pain and doubt!

That day, I asked God a question: "Father, what do you want to show me now that you couldn't before?" I got the answer that evening. I am going out for my evening walk under the stars with Bella, my dog, and as I am looking up into the beautiful night sky, He began to speak to me the sweetest words. Words that changed my life!

"I want to be your husband; I want to be your dad. I want to be the one to make you feel safe. I want to be the one who takes care of you." Well, the answer couldn't have been clearer. This is what God wants for me right now. Oh, how my heart was touched. I had a dad. I had a husband, and I am safe now. I have someone who wants to take care of me. I felt light as a feather! I had no reason to worry anymore as I stood in the midst of the aftermath this storm had brought to my life.

God walks on the clouds, and He is aware of the storms. He knows intimately about my storm. That night changed everything. I was dancing at that moment with Jesus, and it was the sweetest dance ever.

I want you to realize something important. Maybe it is why you were led to this book, maybe it is the message you need in your life right now. God knows you, and He knows what you need. He knows what you want. In order for your heart to be healed, your heart must come under the care of the Great Physician. He does not want to break us, but He does want to break off the darkness around your heart. He wants to bring light to your heart to dispel those lies. Change may be necessary, but it's only so that God can bring light. Some things, my friend, only Jesus can do. They say time heals everything, but I'm sorry, time does not heal things. If you leave a wound and wait for time to pass without treating the symptoms, it will likely become infected. If you put that same wound under the light, open it up, and clean it out, healing will occur. In Jesus' best loving way, He allows change to come. It may come from anywhere, and it may surprise you, but know this: it will affect you for the rest of your life if you accept it. Just sit with Him, lie before Him, and He will speak truth to you as far back as you need to go. Release the memory of your pain and dysfunction. Remember, you are dancing with Jesus. You can trust Him to lead.

So, as you continue in your walk and allow God to have His way, you will begin to see that this is not happening to you, but it is happening for you. He loves you more than you know and wants the best for you. He wants to be your dad, and He wants to be Ishi. Which means, your husband." Yes, it is an actual word in the second chapter of Hosea. Read this beautiful story of a woman who went after other loves only to come up short. God watched as this happened also to Israel, and how His people chose other gods and did not trust His promises. It goes on to say that even though they forgot the Lord, He allured her and led her into the wilderness and spoke tenderly to her. He went after his people! He used this story in the Bible to show us His love for us. He gave her back her inheritance and made her door of pain into a door of hope.

"That day, He declares over her, you will call me 'Ishi,' my husband, you will no longer call me my master."[6] God made a covenant with them; to protect them so they could lie down in safety. "I will betroth you to me forever, in righteousness and justice and love and compassion. I will betroth you in faithfulness and you will acknowledge the Lord."[7] He is extending His love and faithfulness to an unfaithful people because He loved them. He loved them first!

It was "time" to know He is my "Ishi." I'll tell you an interesting story about the same time this awful storm hit my house. My sweet grandson came over often, and I had this beautiful goldfish that just kept getting bigger and bigger. Well, my grandson loved to look at him, and I never could come up with a name for this fish, so I just called him fishy. One night, my grandson was there, and he couldn't pronounce fishy, and out of his mouth came the words, Ishi. At the moment, I thought it was cute, but the next day it dawned on me that I had an Ishi living in this house with me. Ishi, my goldfish, had been there a long time. Ishi the goldfish had several lives. He jumped out of his tank one day, and my son saw him lying on the table and saved him. He had been saved on several different accounts. He was a funny conversation, that fish. The whole thing tickled me, and you know I believe God has a great sense of humor, and He will use just about anything to let us know that He is watching over us. He speaks loudly at times and sometimes uses a child, and sometimes a beautiful goldfish.

What am I trying to say? Is there more to this story to think about? What if Jesus wants to be your Ishi? What if Jesus wants to be your husband even if you have a husband? John 4:4 tells the story of the woman at the well, who had five husbands, and Jesus told her none of those men were her husband. He told her the man you are with now is not your husband. Jesus wanted to share something that day with the Samaritan woman, and I believe He wants all women to know it. We have an Ishi; we have a husband who cares for us. We are not alone, and we can live our lives knowing we are safe; we have a husband. If you have a husband who lives with you and you do life together, then you have a gift. A gift that shouldn't be taken lightly. We know we aren't promised forever here on this earth with our loved ones, but we are promised to have a husband forever. Jesus is our husband. He sits at the well, waiting for women to come to draw water, and as you draw from Him, He will pour His life into our souls. Jesus, the lover of my soul and yours, wants to be first in our lives. I hope you understand the importance of what I am saying. He wants to be first!

I think about those two words I heard that morning when God woke me up and said, "It's time." My storm was raging, and He wanted me to know I had favor and compassion. No more "ashes for food and no more tears mingled in my drink." He wanted me to know that He is my husband. It is comforting as a woman to know that we have Jesus, the lover of our soul, our husband, right by our side at all times. So, whether the road leads through the valley or wherever it takes you, don't question it. Just trust Him. Jesus is bringing you to a place where He can speak tenderly to you. That, my friend, is the best place to be!

Forty Minutes vs. Forty Days

I'm so glad you are still here with me. That tells me you want to dance. If you are going to dance with Jesus, you might need to lighten your load. Imagine a couple on the dance floor moving around with a backpack on their shoulders. Yes, a backpack! There is nothing graceful about dancing with a backpack on your shoulders, but that's exactly what you might appear to Jesus as you bear the weight of the world.

As human beings, we worry and feel guilty. We want to fix things and make everyone happy. The list goes on, and we all carry burdens we are not meant to bear. Can you let go of the worry, stress, and control to live a life of freedom? Will you empty your backpack, so your soul is free to dance? Yes, it is possible to dance with a backpack on your shoulders, but the dance is much better without it. If you don't shed the baggage, there will be nothing beautiful or graceful about your dance.

Let's take a look at our backpacks and see what needs to be removed.

In 1 Samuel 17, David, the son of Jesse, receives strict orders from his father to go to the battlefield and check on his brothers. He is bringing them food and bringing back word to their father about what is happening. David sets out on his mission with his backpack filled with provisions for a half-day journey. When he gets there, he finds the Israelite army gathered in a valley, all huddled together. He searches for his brothers, and when he finds them, he begins to ask them questions. His brothers immediately confront him, wanting to know what he is doing there. David pays them no mind and is more intent on seeing what is happening because he is on a mission to bring back a report to his father. He notices the commotion in the valley and sees how his brothers and the Israelite army sit around, anxious and fearful.

There's a valuable lesson for all of us right there, my friend! If you're feeling anxious or fearful, you might be in a valley yourself, perhaps in the clutches of a giant. It's not God! He does not want us to have a spirit of fear.

As David is speaking with his brothers, out of nowhere appears a nine-foot giant with the voice of a grizzly bear; his name is Goliath. This giant is insulting and mocking the army of God. Goliath's actions were intended to intimidate the Israelites, and sadly, it was working. But a young boy, named David, was there, and he had more passion in his little finger than all his brothers put together. David wasn't afraid of this giant, but he was greatly distressed at the treatment Israel was receiving. David didn't back down. He was ready to take down the giant. Word got back to King Saul, who was hiding in his tent, that someone in the camp was willing to fight Goliath. Up to this point, no one had come forward. King Saul spoke with David, and David told the King he was the one who could take down this giant. Even though it seemed doubtful, King Saul didn't argue with him; he was desperate. It had been forty days, and King Saul couldn't find anybody brave enough to go up against the giant.

A young shepherd boy who had fought off bears and lions while tending sheep in the field was going to take down a giant that had bullied this army for forty days. King Saul brought David into his tent and began to dress him in armor to prepare him for battle with the giant. He placed a bronze helmet on David's head and strapped a sword to his side. Dressed for battle and probably wearing armor for the first time, David turned to King Saul and appealed to him. "I cannot even walk in this outfit. King Saul, I cannot go out in this armor." So David took it off, grabbed his staff, and walked out to face the giant. He stooped down, picked up five smooth stones, put them in his shepherd's bag, and prayed to God. David was not a giant of a man, but rather a small boy, and he was not armed with a sword, but with a stone.

The difference is that David is carrying something more along with those five stones; he carries the authority that comes from his faith. The Philistines laughed at the sight of a small boy walking onto the battlefield to face Goliath. But things change when they see Goliath fall to the ground. One small stone aimed at the giant struck him right in the forehead. All it took was one stone for David to take down Goliath. David wasn't finished, though; he then took the sword from Goliath's side and beheaded him with his own weapon. The Philistine army ran in fear. They were defeated by the faith and courage of a young boy. If that doesn't get you excited, then you might want to check your pulse.

David, in the name of the Lord, slayed the giant. The moral of the story is that God doesn't need our help to defeat a giant, but He does need our cooperation. That is why He invites you to dance with Him. He needs you to partner with Him. Will you let Jesus lead the dance? Will you leave the fighting to Him? Are you ready to see some giants fall? This will be the defining moment in your life! Will you retreat like the army of Israel did, or will you be like David? Will you be brave enough to take off the backpack and look inside for the giants that may be holding you back from your victory, and cooperate with Jesus to annihilate all of them?

Giants come in all shapes and sizes, but the giant of fear is the most prevalent. Why? It hides well. You can't fight what you can't see. Sometimes we don't realize we're living in fear; it sneaks into our lives. A good question to ask yourself is, "What am I afraid of?" Is it a fear of failing? If so, did you know that every success story always involves failure, and sometimes more than one? I love Thomas Edison's attitude. He said, regarding his invention of the light bulb, "I have not failed 10,000 times.

I have not failed once. I have succeeded in proving that those 10,000 ways will not work. When I eliminate the ways that will not work, I will find the way that will work." Don't you love that!

Maybe you are afraid of being alone? You bite the apple if you think you are alone, and so did I. It is a lie straight from the pit of hell. You are surrounded by God everywhere you go; read the scriptures and see how many times God told His leaders, "Do not be afraid," because He was right there. It's easy to bite that apple, but remember, you are not alone.

The giant of rejection is deadly and crippling, and it far overstays its welcome. Trust me, it stayed too long in my life. Rejection is a giant that many people have endured, but I want you to consider something. How can we claim to be rejected when God knew us before we were formed in our mother's womb and wrote our story long before we got here? Furthermore, He chose us before the foundation of the world to bring Him glory in our lives. Oh, I know it's hard to see past the pain of rejection. It's difficult to move beyond how someone treated you. I understand, but the day I realized that I was made and created long before my parents decided to have children, everything changed for me. Value returned to my life, and worth, yes, worth took on a new meaning. You may still feel triggered by this giant of rejection, but once you see the light and recognize that you are loved and valued, purpose will begin to bloom and help you stand right back up!

Complacency is a giant to which we can easily succumb; the comforts of life can hold you back from pursuing your dreams. Ask yourself, are you settling? Are you living the abundant life that Jesus talks about? I brought my questions to God and asked Him to help me confront the truth and to be brave enough to stand up for what I believe in. You don't want to be a victim of your complacency your whole life; you want to live! You don't want to settle; you want God's best for you!

The giant of anger is one that people can become so blinded by, and if it isn't dealt with, it will destroy its victim. We need to pray and ask God, "Are we angry about anything?" Just wait; He will tell you! Anger doesn't hurt anyone but you! Anger in your body can increase health risks due to constant stress, and it will gradually destroy your body and your relationships. So, how do we rid ourselves of anger? Anger is often born of bitterness. Perhaps someone hurt you, did you wrong, and you need to forgive them. How do we do that? I have asked God that question myself. "Lord, I want to forgive, but how do I forgive?" He answered, "Pray for the one who hurt you." By doing so, I learned you can't be angry at someone you are praying for God to bless. Releasing bitterness and anger is liberating. When I forgave, I experienced a sense of freedom. Once you experience letting go and forgiving someone, your joy is restored. So pray! The Bible says to "Pray for your enemies."[1] Do this, and you can be free from anger.

Addiction, discouragement, intimidation, resentment, doubt, jealousy, and guilt can also be giants in your life. Any one of them can wrap their tentacles around your heart and mind. Discouragement is particularly deadly. I believe this is a tactic the enemy uses when he wants to stop a child in their progress toward a stronger relationship with God. When he sees someone fervently pursuing God, he despises that and will do everything possible to aim an arrow and strike where it hurts. He will use a person or a situation to sow disappointment and discourage you. The enemy wants to keep you captive and weigh you down. He does not wish for you to be free, nor does he want you to pursue your purpose. He seeks to prevent you from becoming who God created you to be.

We must be real to ourselves and our Father when we are asking Him to free us. Scripture says, "If we confess our sins, He is just and will forgive us our sins."[2] Sometimes our prayer needs to be three words, "Lord, help me."

We aren't going to do this alone. David didn't face this challenge by himself; he called on the name of the Lord to help him defeat that giant.[3] So, for instance, if fear is holding you back, you need to seek scripture about fear and stand on it every time you feel the enemy and his tentacles suffocating you. I mean, stand on it! Perhaps you're wondering what she means by "Standing on a Scripture?" Take the Word of God, find a scripture in the Bible about fear that resonates with you, and whenever you sense fear, call upon that scripture and remind yourself of the truth. If you have to do it every five minutes, do it! Over time, you will start to see the fear diminish right before your eyes.

From the day I was born, rejection has sought to destroy me. Guilt followed me around like a ball and chain as a young girl, and I wished I had a dollar for every time I told my mom I was sorry. She would always say to me, "Sorry for what?" I didn't know what I was sorry for; I just felt like something was wrong. She always comforted me; she was the best mother, and I loved her so much. After discovering how my birthday unfolded, I now understand why I felt this way in my heart. Something was wrong, and I was just too young to understand. I don't know why my dad thought he needed a boy that day in the hospital, but he got a daughter. Guilt wrapped itself around me, and insecurity followed me for a very long time. It has also taken a long time to unravel all this, because growing up in such an environment planted a seed that went to the depths of my soul, and the message was that I was not valuable. I was not special.

On top of that, my idea of what a father looks like also became twisted. That's why I want you to clean out that backpack and not wait another day. I do not want it to take you as long as it took me to find the truth. It is no accident that you are reading my book. Please know that the Father loves you just the way you are, and He wants you to have a great life. I read the Word of God every day, and I eventually broke free from everything that entangled me. God's Word brought life to me and exposed the lie. One scripture can change everything. I am not here to point fingers at my dad's behavior; I am here to point fingers at the enemy. The enemy is cruel. He used my dad and his desire for a son to begin the task of destroying me. I will not, and I hope you will not, be offended by what others do against you; sometimes, they have no idea that the enemy is using them. Harboring those feelings in your heart only hurts you. I will not excuse that behavior either; they are wrong, and it hurts. After now seeing God's love for me, all that does is fuel the fire in me that there must be something in me that the enemy wanted to destroy. God will not waste anything but will use it for good in your life. Do yourself a favor and find in the scriptures how much you are valued and loved, and believe it. Choose to believe the Bible over the lie. That is what I mean by standing on a verse!

As we grow older, we often become complacent and think it's too late to make a change, but God is our sustainer, and if He has a plan for you, He intends for you to follow through. "For whoever wants to save their life will lose it, but whoever loses their life for me and the gospel will save it."[4] Following Jesus can sometimes place you in uncomfortable situations; the cross alone that He carried for us was something none of us could endure. It was uncomfortable, to say the least. To do the Father's will, you and I will need to step out of our comfort zone. Please don't give it a second thought and retreat, because I assure you that following God and dancing with Him is worth it all. Discovering how much you are loved and how valuable you are can change your life. It changed mine. Moving from feeling unworthy to experiencing Him and allowing Him to show you your worth will leave you excited about each new day. Your best days are ahead. You will be astonished by how God will use the circumstances in your life, and He will walk with you and heal you. He will speak the truth to you. You may think, "I'll be like this forever, living in self-loathing and defeat," but I'm here to tell you how awesome God is. Psalm 139 tells us that even the hairs on our heads are numbered. He knows everything about you. The message of this verse to His sons and daughters is to let us know how close we are to His heart. Chosen by Him, handpicked by Him, with access to all the good things God has in store for us!

The giants that have haunted us our whole lives will shatter when we choose a path with God. When we allow God to break that outer shell, He can come in and reveal His love, shining light into our souls so that we become who we were meant to be. Sure, it may not be easy at first, and the transformation may take longer than forty days, but it will happen. I promise. I am one of those who lived in the ashes of defeat my entire life, and self-loathing is something very real; I can attest to that. Thank goodness Jesus is in the transformation business. I am a miracle, a walking testimony, and I know it! I wouldn't have gotten this far without His Living Word. Standing on a scripture you know He has given you is an experience you will never forget. A warrior is born in such an environment, and that's what we were created to be – warriors!

The verse that birthed vision into my life was Isaiah 61:1-4, "The Spirit of the Lord is on me because the Lord has anointed me to preach good news to the poor. He has sent me to bind up the brokenhearted, to proclaim liberty for the captives, and to release from darkness for the prisoners. To proclaim the year of the Lord's favor and the day of vengeance of our God, to comfort all who mourn and provide for those who grieve in Zion. To bestow on them a crown of beauty instead of ashes, the oil of gladness instead of mourning, and a garment of praise instead of a spirit of despair. They will be called oaks of righteousness, a planting of the Lord, for His splendor. They will rebuild the ancient ruins and restore the places long devastated; they will renew the ruined cities that have been devastated for generations."

Can you see God's plan in those verses for you, your children, and your children's children? Look closely and know that He wants to give you a crown of beauty for those ashes and joy instead of mourning. He desires to help you rebuild. You could be the catalyst for turning things around in your family, breaking generational curses for those who will follow. You will witness God rebuild the ruins that the enemy has come to destroy. God wants to help you and provide you with a vision. That is the good news!

I'm asking you to take a step, unpack your backpack, and talk to God like you would to your best friend. I promise you, things in your life will start to change. I asked Him all the time when I was at the peak of my struggles, and He always provided me with encouragement along the way.

I went shopping recently. As I strolled through the store, I whispered a prayer. Overcome by a feeling of sadness, I needed strength, so I quietly asked for God's help. While driving home, I felt certain that God had touched me. Although I don't remember the exact moment, I knew I was feeling better. I felt okay. The heaviness had lifted, and joy began to return! Joy is so different from happiness. We may not always experience seasons of happiness, but we can still have joy. It lies deep within every child of God. We must ask God to restore our joy, and He will. Our joy is our strength, my friend!

Speaking of joy, as I write this chapter, it is Christmas. In Matthew, chapter 1, the angel gives Mary and Joseph instructions about Christ's birth and how He would be born of a virgin. His name shall be called Emmanuel, which is interpreted as "God with us."[5] God is with you! You will never face a situation alone; He is living inside you and is doing life right beside you.

I leave you with something to think about. David killed a giant in less than forty minutes. The Israelites endured a giant who bullied them for forty days, and some of us, including myself, have sadly allowed them to remain for as long as forty years, but those days are over. I am living my best life after cleaning out my backpack, and I want to encourage you that the sooner you silence those giants, the sooner you, too, will be on a path to living your best life. Go slay some giants today!

You Know My Name

S ometimes, usually when you don't see it coming, a "suddenly" can happen in your life, leaving you feeling completely out of control. They occur, and you could probably compare it to free-falling from a plane; you don't know which end is up. When this happens, it is a good time to say, "Catch me, Lord!" In these moments, if He doesn't catch you, the circumstances can hit hard. "Catch me!" It is the prayer He wants to hear from His children, said with total surrender, trust, and the confidence that He will catch you.

I want to tell you about one of those moments—not a "suddenly" sort of moment, but a time when my Father wanted to show me that He was in control. During my morning devotion, I noticed this song on my phone kept appearing whenever I accessed my music. Day after day, every time I opened YouTube, there it was. I was captivated by the title of the song, "You Know My Name."[1] I was also drawn to the cover photo of beautiful mountains that someone had designed to accompany this song. I wasn't familiar with this mountain range, but it was a lovely image for the song. The song would appear often, and I found myself stopping each time to listen, eventually falling in love with the lyrics. You know my name; the title alone drew me in because it felt wonderful to be recognized. The questions we have, along with our wounded souls, go hand in hand; we long to be known. If you've ever faced rejection in your life, then you'll understand this, and you probably have questions, too.

Maybe someone in your life didn't love you the way you needed, or perhaps you felt they didn't want you. Maybe you have experienced abandonment. If you have, I want to pause and say I am sorry that you had to go through this pain. You understand what struggle is, and I empathize with how you feel. Environments like that can wound a soul deeply. God saw it, my friend, and He can heal that wound. Remember, God created us, molding and fashioning us to His liking. He accepted us long before we ever faced rejection or abandonment. He knows my name, and He knows yours; He reminds us in His Word that we belong to Him. Psalms 139 speaks about how much He knows us. He knows everything there is to know about you. Verse 2 says, "He knows when we sit and when we rise and He perceives our thoughts from afar. Before a word is on our tongue, He knows it completely. All the days ordained for you were written in a book before one of them came to pass."[2] You are known, and there is no need to embrace the lie any longer. We hold on to past hurts when God created and accepted us. He wants to take our brokenness and make us brand new. I'm not sure about you, but that sounds really good to me. To trust Him with my life, knowing, as Isaiah the prophet says, there's not a fire that can burn me, no mountain that I can't climb, and no battle that can defeat me. It is a choice we get to make.[3] Will you believe what God says about you? It all hinges on that.

This song, which I kept listening to, encouraged me and reminded me that He holds my hand. Day after day, and for months, I sang this song and learned to sing it by heart. During this time, I received a phone call from my son, Jon, who was telling me about a ranch out West. He had sent an email to this ranch about a job. There was a possibility that he might work on this ranch during the pandemic. This was a beautiful ranch in Jackson, Wyoming, looking for a wrangler. A wrangler is a trail guide who takes groups of people on rides to some of the most breathtaking views. Yes, every day my son could go to work on a ranch, and he was telling me all about it.

Well, no sooner had I gotten off the phone than the wheels started turning. I had always wanted to visit a dude ranch out west. I've loved horses since I was two years old, and I wanted to get out there with one, one way or the other. So, I called him back and started sharing how great it would be if I could visit and take a trail ride with him. He got tickled about this and told me to let him get the job first, and we would figure out my visit later. We still laugh about that call.

Sure enough, it happened. My son drove 24 hours across the country to fulfill a dream of living on a ranch as a wrangler. He led people on beautiful trails, climbing steep mountains, crossing rivers, and keeping an eye out for wild animals. He met some great people, and he didn't mind if I followed right behind him and joined him. Of course, he got permission from his boss, and as soon as he did, I booked a plane ticket. Living on a working ranch and waking up at dawn was an experience of a lifetime. I helped saddle sixty to eighty horses a day before breakfast. I was pinching myself the whole time. I thought about Psalm 139 as I lived this dream and said to myself, "God opened this door for me and Jon because He knows us!" I was reminded daily of the words of that song. It was no accident that the song popped up on my phone months ago; He ordained it. Yes, He knows us, and He knows just what we love to do, and it was written down long before we lived it.

I flew into Jackson Hole, Wyoming. It feels like a hole because you are surrounded by mountains when you land on this tiny airstrip. When I stepped off the plane, I saw this view! I couldn't believe my eyes! Before me were the infamous Grand Teton Mountains that I had been staring at on my phone for the last few months, and I had no idea where they were until that day. I walked down the ramp from the plane, just shaking my head and smiling all the way. Yes, smiling! Free-falling is not so bad after all, I began to think. Difficult seasons are always the best time to say, "Catch me, Father." I decided that day I would let Jesus toss me up on the dance floor whenever He wanted. I was overwhelmed by God's love. He was trying to send me a wonderful message of His love for me. He knew I was trying so hard to trust Him.

My son, Jon, picked me up at this rustic-looking, cowboy airport, wearing his boots and cowboy hat, grinning like a horse eating briar, and off we headed to this cowboy's dream. Oh, it gets better, you see, because in this photo I had been looking at for months, I didn't even notice that there was something else in the picture. I sometimes forget to zoom in and see everything God wants to show me. It comes as a surprise later.

The day I arrived, I showed Jon this picture. I told him I had been singing this song, and he looked at it. He did what most millennials do—he zoomed in. That's when he pointed out something I hadn't seen. Jon said, "Yeah, Mom, that barn you see there is also in Jackson. It's one of the most photographed barns in the world." I sat there staring at him, wondering what he was talking about. "What barn?" I asked as we drove along. All those months I'd stared at that picture, there was a barn I hadn't noticed. Yes, the most photographed barn in the world is in Jackson, Wyoming, and it was in that picture. You have to know me to understand why a barn would excite me—I practically lived in one my whole childhood. The barn my dad built behind our house was my sanctuary. It was a place to find peace and enjoy the quiet. During those years, I had many questions, and I didn't get all the answers, but I found comfort in that barn. I have always loved horses; we can learn so much from them. God loves to show up and bless His children with the little things we love. He knew the questions pressing on my heart; He was right there with me—I just didn't realize it at the time. I grew up as a cowgirl, and she will never part from me; it's just how He made me. So, part of my life's dance was a ranch out west, filled with everything a cowgirl could dream of. He set it all up for me, and the best part was sharing it with one of my boys. Jon is a cowboy. As a young boy, he always wore a cowboy hat and boots. He loves ranch life and riding horses, too. It was a dream beyond my wildest, and even better, I shared it with him.

So, what about you? Where is God going to take you? If you follow Him, He will lift you up in this dance, catch you, and plant your feet right in a place you love. So, when a "suddenly" comes into your life, hold on—it's just Him moving. Trust Him!

That's just one of my stories about how He surprised me that day as I stepped off the plane. It was a chance to live on a ranch and take in some of the most breathtaking views. I met some of the sweetest people who treated me like family, and I shared an old log cabin with Jon. That was priceless. We spent a day together at Yellowstone National Park and saw some beautiful sights—bison grazing so close we could have touched them, a grizzly momma bear with her cub. We also got to visit that famous barn. God is good!

Experiencing life on a ranch out west was a dream come true for me. He knew my name, and He knew what would make me smile. This is an exciting time for you because dancing with Jesus is real. He knows your name too, and you know what else? He knows all the little things that will make you smile as well.

Dancing in the Dark

The title alone sounds exciting and fun, right? Of course, that's just that crazy side of me, but honestly, I believe we all have a little bit of that side deep down. We don't use it often enough, or we don't use it at all, which sometimes makes us think that it doesn't exist within us.

Some things we read in the Old Testament that God asked people to do seem a little crazy, too. Think about Moses and what God asked him to do. I'm paraphrasing, but this is essentially what God told Moses: "Moses, stand before the Red Sea, hold up your staff, stretch out both arms because I am going to make a path right through it so the Israelites can pass over to the other side."[1] That sounds like it was pretty adventurous. Moses was definitely up for the challenge! He probably needed something exciting, since he had to deal with the Israelites complaining all the time. And remember when Jesus told Peter to step out of the boat onto the water and walk to Him, even in the middle of a raging storm? Peter was probably one of those risk-takers, and Jesus knew it. He asked Peter because He knew Peter. Let's not forget little David, the shepherd boy who took five stones and a sling, walked up to a giant, and took him down. He did pray, no doubt, but you could say they had a small dance together, and it left the whole community speechless.

Compared to these biblical stories, dancing with Jesus doesn't seem too crazy. Right? I'm a bit of a chicken, but adventure is a different story! I like doing exciting things, and going to the edge has always intrigued me. We are all created so differently. Some people enjoy adventure, while others are content just looking at pictures. However, I believe sometimes we get too comfortable with living and may lose touch with our adventurous side. We might need something to happen to shake things up a bit. In fact, walking out to the edge is how I feel I am walking these days. I am dancing in the dark, which means I have no idea where He is taking me; but I must be honest and say I have never felt more alive. I also know Jesus will only lead me to places that will be good for me. That is the kind of God we serve. Jesus is genuinely looking out for your good. If you believe that, then fear and anxiety will lose their hold on you.

It reminds me of the story of Abraham and Isaac, which takes place in Genesis 17. Abraham and Sarah were married, but they didn't have any children. Of course, they wanted children, but Sarah couldn't conceive, the Bible says.[2] So, she did what many women might do—although not me. I don't think I would have ever agreed to share my husband with another woman, but that's just me. I'm laughing as I type because I know myself too well. Times were different then, and Sarah agreed to have Hagar, her maidservant, lie with Abraham; she wanted him to have a child, so she went to great lengths to help God out. That was her first mistake! God doesn't need our help in any matter. Nine months later, Abraham and Hagar had a son, whom Abraham named Ishmael. Abraham and Sarah raised the boy, and everything seemed fine—until a few years later, when Abraham was surprised to have some visitors. Suddenly, a few men—who we could call messengers of God—showed up at his door. Abraham welcomed them into his home and fed them. They had some news to share with Abraham and Sarah, but neither of them was ready for what they were about to hear. They told Abraham that Sarah would become pregnant within the next year and would give birth to a son. Sarah overheard this and started laughing in another room, and they heard her. The funny thing is, it would be pretty hard for us to keep a straight face in that situation; we'd probably laugh too. Imagine that! She was in her nineties, and giving birth to a baby seemed absurd, but Abraham trusted these visitors. So, Sarah lay with Abraham, and she became pregnant, carried the child, and gave birth to a little boy. It all happened just as it was told to Abraham. His name would be Isaac, just as God had said.[3]

Never underestimate the word of God; if He says it, you can count on it! Have you received a Word, or are you standing on a Word right now? It takes time for these things to happen, and like Sarah, we may have to wait. The story continues to show

how Abraham and Sarah loved this child. They loved him so much that Abraham was beginning to do the inevitable, risking the danger of allowing another human to become so close to his heart that they became inseparable. God was concerned and saw this developing in Abraham's heart and knew He had to remove this unhealthy love. We are never meant to depend on another person or to put anyone before God in our hearts. God wants first place. Our devotion must be to Him first because we were created for Him. Nothing—absolutely nothing—and no one should take precedence over our Lord. He is a jealous God. He also knows that nothing good will come from placing anything or anyone before Him. In Matthew 22:36, Jesus tells the disciples, as they ask Him this question, "Teacher, which is the great commandment in the law?" And He said to them, "You shall love the Lord your God with all your heart and with all your soul and with all your mind." That puts a new perspective on many things.

So it happened that God met Abraham and told him to take his son, his only son Isaac, and go to Mount Moriah, a three-day journey, to offer him as a sacrifice to Him.[4] Can you imagine? Abraham was instructed by Almighty God to sacrifice his son, his only son, on an altar. That day would mark the beginning of the struggle. From the moment he heard those words, I believe it was a heavy burden for him to carry. From God's point of view, He was removing a burden that Abraham was never meant to carry. We cannot always see what God sees in the moment. Sometimes we don't even realize that things are out of balance.

We might think everything is normal. But God wants to rescue us from that! Abraham kept this to himself, and the Bible says that the very next morning, he set out on this journey. Talk about obedience! He didn't waste any time! He stood on the Word God had given him—that his seed would come through Isaac! I believe Abraham quickly faced the core of the issue, which was the question, Who do I love more? Have you ever thought about that? Is there a love in your life that, if God asked you that question, what would be your answer? I challenge you to consider what your answer would be. Don't wait for a trial by fire. Ask God to show you where your true 'allegiance' lies. Abraham had to confront it, and I believe we all will face this at some point. It is a simple but important question, so why should we be surprised when God asks us?

This story reminds me of the Father and His Son. God needed a sacrifice for all mankind because of the mess we were in with sin. Jesus willingly gave His life to redeem us; He knew and trusted the Father's plan.[5] Have you ever felt like no one cares about or loves you? Hold on to the fact that God gave His Son to us. John 3:16, "For God so loved the world he gave His only Son Jesus, that whosoever believes in Him shall not perish but have everlasting life." Jesus was willing to be that sacrifice for you. You are loved!

God knew what Abraham would do in that trial because He is omniscient, an all-knowing God. God wanted Abraham to examine his heart and see that things were out of order. God desires the same for us. He wants us to pause and reflect on what is in our hearts. Is anything out of order? Sometimes it is a trial by fire, a circumstance, or situation that God uses to reveal things to us. God told Abraham that Isaac, his offspring, would be blessed, and his seed would be multiplied as the stars in heaven. Nations would come from his seed, and his descendants would overcome their enemies' gates. So, Abraham had to believe that if he offered his son as a sacrifice, God would raise him from the dead right before his eyes. He had to trust the promise! So, he decided to trust God blindly and take Him at His Word![6]

He packed his belongings and told Sarah that he would be taking a trip with Isaac and the servants. By faith, he told Sarah they would all return in a few days. Yes, I was thinking the same thing; that's strong faith. I want to have faith like Abraham—how about you? Abraham declared God's Word and his future with his own words. His story is a powerful lesson for us all! God led Abraham to the very edge, and at one moment, He stopped him. A voice—and I'm sure the sweetest voice Abraham ever heard—came from heaven and told Abraham to STOP! The image in my mind is Isaac lying on the altar, Abraham with a knife in his hand, and his son staring up at him.[7] What Abraham faced was a great trial. It was a fire test for sure! God had to guide him through it so that Abraham could see what was in his heart and remove any unclean love. Hopefully, this story reminds us how important our hearts are to Him.

Sometimes God gives us a word and expects us to act exactly as He has instructed, such as in His written Word provided through the scriptures. We would be wise to pick it up, read it, and follow through. Don't look at your surroundings, don't look to the right or the left; look in His Word and let Him give you the answer you're seeking.

I feel I've experienced the same as Abraham recently. This trial by fire I've gone through has lasted for a few years. It takes some of us a little longer to see what our Father is pointing out, but dancing in the dark is where we begin to see more clearly. The valleys will lead us to the mountaintop. We might not receive a download of information or a specific timeline, but as we are taught in the 23rd Psalm, we walk through the valley! It is dark, but we NEVER pitch a tent there.

I understand that you might hesitate to look into your heart and recognize the human tendencies that have taken hold within it. Sometimes we don't even realize how those tendencies got in there. Remember your commitment to God and be mindful of the blinders. Can you trust Him enough to look, because HE knows?

I want to please Him more than anything; I want to receive everything God has for me. It's major surgery on our hearts, yes, but knowing the Master's hand has held our hearts and touched the places we long for Him to reach— isn't that what we all desire? To remove the unclean love from our hearts? Sin is like a tumor or poison in our bloodstream that will destroy us if it remains inside. If we just let God be God and trust Him in the darkness, we'll become much healthier people.

Today, people spend a lot on supplements and health foods, and we should, but let's not stop there. God shined the light into my heart one day and showed me just a glimpse of how unhealthy my heart had become. It was a sickness of the heart, and my tears were proof. This small wound I had carried all my life grew, and it became an infection that was destroying my very soul. That's right, sickness grows. It had been hiding in my heart for years and was like poison dripping into my bloodstream daily. One small drip of poison a day is just as harmful as drinking a glassful at once; both can kill you. God whispered to me, "It's time," and I believe the Master put me on the operating table. A table of His making; a dance in the dark.

Don't worry, if God sees something bordering on perilous in His children's hearts, He won't just stand by and do nothing. He is in control and works in the hearts and lives of His people. When He comes and points out areas of concern, pay attention. Don't think you're just imagining things. You've heard Him correctly. He speaks softly, but He does speak. The wonderful thing about our Father is that if we don't hear it at first, He will speak again and again and again. Such love! I had known this trial by fire was coming long before it arrived. I didn't hear an audible voice like Abraham, but the Spirit of God is always present, and He lets His children know things before they happen. Things can come suddenly, but sometimes He whispers into our hearts because that's how loving of a Father He is.

As I write these words, I am comforted by His Presence, knowing that this profound suffering and all the sleepless nights

I have endured have not been in vain. He was working something out of my heart, something that was close to the edge of danger — a weight too heavy for me, an infected heart that needed healing. We think differently because we are in the dark, clueless about the most important things. The Word of God says, "to guard your heart, for it is the wellspring of life."[8] I wonder how many people even think about that verse. We go to the doctor if we feel pain. We even undergo annual physicals to maintain our overall health. Look at what we go through just to remove a small splinter. I challenge you to examine your heart, and even better, to have a conversation with God about it. He loves us so much and cares about our spiritual health. He sees everything, and He knows our hearts.

One morning, as I awoke to the sunlight streaming through my window, He spoke to me as I was opening my eyes and He said, "Life is like mining; working in the dark, but Jesus will bring a diamond out of the rough." Oh, I love it when He speaks; He is always right on time. He speaks the truth! Life is like mining, but look at what springs from the dark—diamonds!

I hope you feel challenged to take a peek. I hope you will have that conversation with God about your heart, your health, your marriage, your children, or anything that concerns you. It only takes one sentence to start a conversation—begin one today, my friend. He will answer; all you need to do is be patient. If you're feeling like you're in the dark right now and don't understand what's happening in your life, then it's time to lift your gaze to the heavens. Keep going! Keep dancing, and I promise you, light will come, flowers will bloom, and joy will arrive in the morning because the darkness is as light to Him.

Hindsight is 20/20

Hindsight is 20/20, an old proverb you are likely familiar with, is based on the idea that vision becomes clearer when looking back. I couldn't agree more, and I believe many others share the same sentiment. I bet the prophets and apostles of the Old Testament would agree with us, too.

Now faith is the substance of things hoped for, and the evidence of things not seen, quite the opposite.[1] So, we grow as we go! We walk by faith, as the scriptures command us, and we can look back from time to time and see how God led us through. Our faith grows stronger every day, every year, and every season. As we look back, we see the works of God's hands in our lives.

I shared earlier in a previous chapter how God reached back into the files of my life and brought up a dream I had at age 18. At 57 years old, that dream still remained. Forty years later, I was a stay-at-home mom about to become a flight attendant, bringing with me high hopes of earning my wings. This time, I would be away for a month, and I was officially employed. On the first day, we would take an exam, and if I didn't pass, I would go straight back home. I felt the pressure—the bar was high. Our days were packed with exams, classwork, memory work, drills, and showing up on time every day. If you were late to class, you went home. We all stayed together for a month in a hotel near the training center. We also had a roommate on this adventure, and that was part of the training as well. We needed to be able to build relationships effectively.

The task was a little overwhelming for a stay-at-home mom, but I stepped onto the dance floor and I danced. One half of me was away from home and in training, while the other half was holding my endless emotions together. You know the song "Amazing Grace;"[2] it was an amazing grace moment by moment for me. I had a mountain of emotions to climb every morning before I even got to the classroom. If we could have shared around the room, I'm sure all kinds of stories led each of us to this moment, and I had quite a story to share. Most of the trainees were young, starting on this journey, and maybe just passing an exam was the only thing on their plate; you never know what the person right next to you may be going through. While all my new friends came packed with every accessory they may need, my suitcase looked a little different. Giants of rejection, insecurity, and a broken heart were what filled my bags. Giants that needed to be slayed, and I was doing my best to do just that. Needless to say, it wasn't easy pulling that suitcase around the airport, but I got to my destination, unpacked, and started work. Lurking over my shoulder daily, those giants let me know they would be joining me on this endeavor as well. Fear was committed to the job and met me as I showed up for training. I showed up, though! I knew in the deepest trenches of my heart that if I showed up, so would God. If I could concentrate, learn from what's in front of me, and be present and secure throughout each day, I knew I would be making progress. "One day at a time" was a quote on my refrigerator door at home, and I reminded myself of that every day. Stretching beyond your comfort zone is not only about being courageous, but also about being curious. When we can cross that line, growth begins.

I met my Father early every morning in a quiet spot in our hotel. Every day, He showed up for me, too. He came with His presence, sometimes with a verse, maybe with a song in my heart, and sometimes He would allow someone to minister to me. A kind word from a stranger can go a long way. God can send the exact word at the precise moment we need to hear it. I was consistently seeking God because I knew I could not go through this journey alone.

We were nearing the end of our four weeks; I had passed all my exams and was on track to earn my wings. In a few days, I would graduate. I had already been assigned my base, received my uniforms, and was beginning a new chapter. As all this was happening, I continued to take one step at a time and trusted God. I was scared. One vulnerable evening with the Lord, I started praying and told Him that if He thought I could do this, I would trust Him with the next step. The next morning, I walked to class confident in what I had told God, trusting Him because I knew He had me! After that prayer, everything changed. I could say it just came out of nowhere, but this time, it seemed to emerge directly from China. The pandemic that shut down the world came quickly, and one of the first things to shut down was the airline industry. Within 48 hours, God had me on a plane heading back to my home in North Carolina. I knew my Father was controlling everything in my life and was stepping in now because, my friend, He controls it all—the universe, our times, your day, and the plans He has for you! He controls it all! It was like He spoke and said, "No further." He may let you walk to the edge, but no further. He spoke to Abraham as he held the knife over Isaac, about to sacrifice him. God came at the moment Abraham needed Him, and He came when I needed Him.

I must admit I was the happiest of all the flight attendants to go home. My classmates were upset, and rightly so; we were days away from graduation, and their dreams were put on hold. All this moved my heart, but I couldn't say a word; I just pondered it all in my heart. I knew the prayer I had prayed a few nights before, and I knew He heard me. So when all this happened, I thanked Him for answering my prayer. I thanked Him for being such a good Father to me. I am here to report that He will never give you more than you can handle. My God took me as far as He needed to, then He pulled me back and brought me home.

When you surrender to Him, there is no need to worry; He is watching over you.

The year 2020 was a time of resting in God's presence. Looking back, He changed everything on a dime when I prayed. I am comforted, knowing I am Daddy's little girl. He provided for me in every way.

Going home was neither difficult nor disappointing; I had my children and grandchildren with me. I was surrounded by family and friends. I had my dog, Bella. I had my church family and my barn family. I also had Jake, a very special horse. But most of all, I had Jesus. Each moment of the day, and every morning when I woke up, He was there. During a time of turmoil in the world, I reflect on what He did for me. I felt like a daughter of a king, living in a castle with armed guards all around. He knew I wasn't ready for that role; I was still so broken. His incredible grace alone kept me together.

God sees everything, and He sees you, my friend, so you can trust Him. As I mentioned, the Word of God states in 1 Corinthians 10:13 that He will put no more on you than you can bear —a promise to hold onto when you feel stretched beyond your limits. Trust me, you can stretch, and it might seem beyond your limits, but He knows you, created you, and understands what you can endure. Trust Him and believe with all your heart that He will not burden you more than you are able to bear.

So, my friend, as you dance this magnificent dance with him, and He decides to throw you in the air, or like me, on a plane, let Him! He has blessings for you. For me, God was teaching me to be brave and gain confidence. I would not have grown in these areas if I had not followed through with that dream. I realized when I finally got home and settled in what I had just accomplished with God's help. I was proud of that moment and proud of myself for stepping out in faith. I saw the hand of God in the journey. Psalm 138 speaks about His right hand saving us. I felt His gentle hand on my life during those weeks of training. I would have never known how strong I could become if I had not followed Him. I also learned that He will sometimes push the pause button in our lives. He wanted to spend time with me and take care of me. He wanted me to see that He was my husband and my dad. Looking back, that is precisely how I see it!

Today, I am back at Topsail Island, and these beautiful continuous waves I see right now keep reminding me of His endless Love for me. If I follow Him and do not try to understand everything all at once, God will guide my path. I don't need to fear dark seasons or deep water. I also don't need to keep treading water or trying to figure things out; I just need to realize I can float! That's right, in 2020 I learned I can float, and no matter how deep the water is, I don't have to worry. When we float, our gaze can only be heavenward. Stop fixating on the situation. Take it to Jesus and rest in the assurance He will not let you fall. Touch your chin with your hand and do what I sometimes do—tilt it upward so your eyes are on Heaven.

Choose to adjust your lens and change your focus! It can be that simple.

One morning, as I was driving to church and talking with my Father, an extraordinary experience happened. Suddenly, one of my hands gently lifted off the steering wheel and instinctively touched my chin, lifting it about an inch. I immediately knew it was the Lord speaking to me. I'll never forget that moment, which is why I share it with you. I encourage you to do the same whenever you catch yourself looking down or focusing on circumstances—they're just passing moments, not permanent. Today, I came to the beach to write for this reason: I needed a reminder of how mighty my God is. Reflecting on the past few months and everything I've achieved, I recognized that His mighty hand guided me every step of the way. Just as His hand was with Moses and Aaron as they led God's people out of Egypt, He will hold your hand, too.

One year to the day after that layoff, we were called back to work, and I would have to start training all over again. I could see my wings in the distance, and I was ready. During that year with God's help, the work in my soul that needed to be done was completed. I was prepared for the next chapter. As I returned to training, I planned to graduate, earn my wings, and begin working as a flight attendant, but His plan for me was to go through that training, pass each drill with confidence, make lasting friendships, and yes, cross that finish line and pin on my wings. He wanted me to see that I could do anything with

Him, but something had also changed that year. The world had changed a lot in just one year, and thankfully, so had I.

Graduation day arrived! It was the moment I pinned on my wings, but this time, the wings meant something different. Each flight attendant received their wings, and they pinned them on with the dream of flying the friendly skies. For me, pinning on my wings went much deeper. Remember, I was broken, and a few months earlier, I had written a song where the words said that He would mend my wings. "My broken wings He would mend because I was made to fly." That year, I had been obedient, sitting with my Father and trusting Him in the deepest waters, earning wings of a different kind. The message I heard that day was that my wings were no longer broken; my wings were healed. My broken wings had been touched by the Hand of the Master, and now I was ready to soar, dance, and fly higher and higher into all the places He has for me. I am going to live the story He wrote for my life. Oh, it was such a moment, sharing it with my Father during that graduation ceremony. As I held those wings in my hand, I knew I was holding destiny, and I proudly pinned them on.

The pandemic changed the world, and it changed the airline industry. Sitting with my Father that year changed me, and 2020 gave my life new meaning. My home was calling me. My grandchildren think I hung the moon—that's how much they love me—and I wanted to be near them. "Present and secure" is airline terminology that's very important in the industry, and those two words became especially meaningful to me. I had been present in my children's lives, and I wanted the same for my grandchildren. I came home confident in my decision not to be away from my family. I had never been apart from them. I'm grateful for all I experienced to earn my flight attendant wings, but my priorities shifted during the pandemic. I wasn't willing to make the sacrifice of being away from my family. God is good. He knew about that desire I had at 18 years old, and He let me check it off my bucket list at 57 years old.

I'm proud of the wings that God helped me earn, and they lie in my jewelry box where I can see them and be reminded of my achievements. I deeply respect the airline industry for the hard work and training they provide to protect the lives of others. During that journey, I made new friends and created memories I will cherish forever. I am thankful for the love and support from my family and friends. They loved and prayed for me, knowing it was a big mountain to climb, but they believed in my ability to succeed—even when I wasn't sure. I felt their prayers every day. There are no words to fully express my gratitude for having such special people in my life. I know I couldn't have done it without their prayers and encouragement.

God did all this for me. He gave me the most wonderful experience a mother of four boys could ever have in this world. I had only imagined it before. He let me reach the edge, then He moved and stepped in, pressing the pause button on my life. He sat me down beside Him, took care of me, and healed me. Why did He do this? I know He did it because I am His little girl, and hindsight truly is 20/20!

Breaking or Becoming

Have you ever read about new wine referenced in the Bible? There are many scriptures that refer to new wine, found in both the Old and New Testaments. I want to speak to you from both. New Wine in the Strong's Concordance is the word *tirosh*, meaning freshly pressed grape juice, not yet fermented.[1] New wine also symbolizes a new spirit, a new beginning, a transformative experience, like the process of turning grapes into wine. Grapes have to be pressed, and the process takes a while so that all the juices are extracted. Interesting! We also know diamonds are created under pressure. From this, we learn that pressure produces fine things.

In the New Testament, Luke 5:33-38, Jesus was questioned by Pharisees and the teachers of the law about why his disciples didn't fast. While the Pharisees and the leaders of the law fasted, Jesus' disciples continued to eat and drink. Jesus was likely waiting for this question to come up, and He answered them,

"Until the Bridegroom is taken away, there is no need to fast."
He then shared that no one tears a patch from a new garment
to sew it on an old one. If he does, he will have torn the new
garment, and the patch from the new will not match the old
garment. And no one pours new wine into old wineskins. If he
does, the new wine will burst the skins, the wine will run out,
and the wineskins will be ruined. New wine must be poured
into new wineskins. Jesus was making one of the most profound
statements of His ministry at this time. He was sharing about
the New Covenant that He was bringing to us. He knew that
when He sacrificed His life for us on the cross, it would bring
new life—a New Covenant to replace the Old Covenant. This
New Covenant will not be like the Old Covenant, which was
based on religious practices, a system of sacrifices, the Levitical
Priesthood, or adherence to the Mosaic Law. That was the Old
Covenant, and it was how they maintained their relationship
with God. There were many duties with the Old Covenant, but
no more sacrifices; Jesus was going to be the ultimate sacrifice.
There was no need to focus on the duties in the Temple because
we are the Temple! Jesus came to earth to provide a simpler
pathway to Him—no more living by Mosaic law, but living a
life of faith. I can feel you relaxing as I am when I read this good
news. That is the Gospel! The Good News!

Since learning about Jesus as a child, I have always harbored
a hunger and desire to know God. As I matured, my wish was
to really know Him and be a close friend who walks with Him.
I read about Enoch in the Old Testament, who walked with

God so intimately that when it was his time to leave this earth, Enoch simply disappeared. The Bible states that he was taken by God, as recorded in Genesis 5:21-24. If Enoch could have such a relationship with God, I wanted that too. As a young girl, I remember thinking that I might not feel important, but if I followed Jesus, I knew everything would turn out well. I saw myself as someone with no gifts or talent, but I had a deep desire to make a difference and leave a legacy. I believed that with Jesus, He would help me fulfill that desire.

Just the other day, I was meditating on Psalm 139 and reached the verse where David says, "How precious to me are your thoughts, O God; how vast is the sum of them!" I began to pray that day and continued throughout, asking Him to share with me His thoughts about me and my life. I wanted to understand them. I truly believe we miss out on so much by not asking Him about the small things that are really the big things. Later that afternoon, I received a message from someone—a dialogue between God and His child. The conversation He was having with His daughter/son was that they are not falling apart, so there's no need to put them back together, but there are pieces that have fallen off. Pieces of darkness. The conversation goes on to say that they are not breaking, but they are becoming—they are becoming who they were created to be. God heard my prayer! I wanted to know His thoughts about me, and He answered. Those were His thoughts toward me. These words are for you too, son or daughter of the Most High—you're not breaking but becoming who you were created to be.

Most people dislike change. They feel it suggests they messed up somewhere along the way. That feeling doesn't sit well with them. When they try hard and then think they didn't succeed, it can be upsetting. I understand! That day, I heard from God in a very personal way. "You are not changing, you are becoming!" We haven't messed up anything! We are becoming who He created us to be!

Jesus teaches in Mark 2:22 that no man can put new wine into old wineskins. Instead, new wine is poured into new wineskins. Oh, it may feel like breaking, but I would rather you remember the process of turning the grapes into wine. Pressure is applied—great amounts of pressure—to squeeze out every ounce of juice from the grape. Transformation requires great pressure. For us to become what God has in mind for us, we need to acquire some new things. We need new ways of living and thinking. Our body and mind cannot hold on to the old and receive the new. The old way of thinking must go. Jesus would say that the Old Covenant has to go for us to embrace the New Covenant! God is breaking off the darkness around you so your light can burst forth.

The Father is so kind, He allows the pressure to be as gentle as He can make it for us. We often don't realize that we are affected by darkness, but when in a dark room, turning on a small light reveals how much easier it is to navigate. Sure, we can feel our way through that darkness if we have to, but why should we? We have access to the light.

So effectively, the surgeon's hand gently removed what I could not. The dark backpack I carried was opened, and God began to shine His light on the guilt I had taken all my life. This giant that entered my life the day I was born would have ultimately destroyed me, but God saw a new and better way for me. The pressure was applied not to hurt me but to heal me. It was a daily process of changing my old mindset, as I had thought it was normal for many years. Giants like that are not of our own making; they come from unhealthy environments. Surgeons are skilled at knowing how to proceed and make necessary corrections to ensure a quick and effective healing process, and we trust them. God is a surgeon too, and when circumstances unfold, we can trust Him as He begins to probe with His skillful hand and remove what is unnecessary. He sees what we cannot see. For some reason, we often have a hard time trusting the unseen surgeon versus the visible doctor in a white coat. Symptoms like pain are present, and God wants to remove them. Any good doctor will tell you that his goal is to improve your quality of life, and our Great Physician, our Creator, desires the same for us. We must trust the process. Does anyone want to sign up to improve their quality of life? What is holding you back?

Let's look at the Old Testament and read how God describes new wine. "Forget the former things; do not dwell on the past. See! I am doing a new thing! Now it springs up; do you not perceive it? I am making a way in the desert and streams in the wasteland."[2] Here, God promises to create a new path for His people in difficult times. He is making a road in the wilderness!

Where there was no way, He made a way! I took His hand and let Him lead me. I cried a lot, but the infection is gone, and healing has come!

In Psalm 31, David cries out to God, "I have become like broken pottery." Even David, at times in his life, felt just like we do. He, too, needed transformation! It is the hand of God that comes into our lives as we invite Him, and He takes what we think is broken and begins the work of transformation in us. It is not something we can do, but God can bring this transformation and renewal to our lives.

I've heard that when things are broken, they often become stronger after being put back together, and I've always wondered if that's true. If it is, I consider myself a very strong woman. I looked into it and found that yes, even when bones break, a callus forms around the fracture, and temporarily, the bone becomes stronger. Of course, it can break again if hit hard enough, but during the healing process, it is stronger than usual. That might help you and me understand how we have gotten through some of our challenges. The exact process that helps a broken bone heal can also be applied to the broken parts of our lives. We survived them, and now we know how.

Jesus, in the Word of God, talks about broken pottery and how the potter, when he needed some clay, would go out to a place where broken pottery was discarded and pick up an old piece of pottery to make something new. Jeremiah 18 describes God as the potter and us as the clay in His hands. "Oh, house of Israel, can I not do with you as this potter has done, declares the Lord? Behold, like the clay in the potter's hand, so are you in my hand, O house of Israel." There is a message for us in the conversation the Father is having with Jeremiah.

Will you let Him sit at the potter's wheel and shape you for His glory? Will you allow Him to take control of your life and fulfill the plans He has for you? These are grown-up questions that demand grown-up answers. My mother used to say, "It is where the rubber meets the road." She was pretty good at coming up with those old sayings people used to say, and more importantly, she lived by them.

I continued my research and discovered something interesting about how things become stronger after they are broken. Kintsugi, a Japanese repair technique, is an art that uses golden lacquer to reassemble broken pottery. Urushi, the traditional Japanese lacquer, is renowned for its exceptional strength and durability, making it an ideal material for repairing pottery. This gold lacquer not only enhances the piece's appearance but also reflects the Japanese appreciation for the beauty of imperfections, adding more value to these items. In Japan, this type of art is highly valued. Yes, something that is broken and then repaired can become even more valuable. Food for thought, right?

I believe this comparison truly changes how we should view things. Did the process of applying urushi to the broken pottery happen overnight? No, it is a process as well. As I looked at the steps, I could see that it went through stages, and it wasn't perfect right away. Life can be just like that, too. God, who created us, desires to see us become what He envisioned long ago, bringing renewal and life to us. There is nothing we need to fix; we are His beloved children. We only need to yield.

Let me explain the process; it's worth hearing: the potter goes to the potter's field and chooses a broken piece of pottery to transform. First, he softens the pottery he selected and kneads it with his hands to prepare it for the potter's wheel. Think about yourself and realize that you are the clay in the potter's hands. He kneads the clay for hours, and when he's satisfied, he places it on the wheel. There, he shapes it into exactly what he has envisioned. He then puts his creation in a kiln at a low temperature to harden the clay. Afterward, he removes it and lets it sit until it cools. He adds a final glaze and places it back in the kiln at a higher temperature. This hardens the glaze, making the pottery strong, waterproof, and ready to use again. The broken piece of pottery that once lay in the potter's field has now become something new. Instead of being discarded, it has a purpose once more.

I hope this encourages you and motivates you to trust the Potter's hand. It is not a one-time event; it takes time. Waiting isn't easy. Sometimes the final result isn't visible. You must trust and believe that it will be good. He is good, and everything He touches becomes beautiful in its time.

I am a piece of clay, and I realize that the old wineskin can't hold the new wine I have become. New things require new containers. My friend, we are not breaking; we are becoming! When God finishes molding and remaking us, we will be a masterpiece in the Kingdom, not to sit idle on a shelf, but to be used for His glory!

New Shoes

D on't you love to get a new pair of shoes? I know I do! I can put on a brand-new pair of shoes with anything in my closet and feel like I'm wearing a new outfit! It's ridiculous, but I know you understand what I'm saying. Well, I feel just as excited with the title of this chapter, New Shoes. Perhaps you are wondering what God is going to share with me about new shoes. All inspiration comes from Him, my friend; so if He doesn't speak, it's just an empty page.

It has been quite a journey thus far, and I am excited about what God has been doing in my heart and life. I am blessed by all He is showing me. I am feeling better, and hope is being manifested in my circumstances. I am a witness to my own transformation. I am starting to see myself differently and think differently. These two changes alone can work wonders for our mental and physical health. The amazing part is knowing who is bringing about this transformation.

It is comforting to look back and recognize who helped us through our trials and tribulations. If only we could go back in time, talk to our younger selves, and share the lessons we learn later in life. One thing we would change is how long we carried the baggage around. God spoke to me the other day and told me to "Get out of my head and follow my heart." He let me know that staying in my head is like staying in a file cabinet of old files that I no longer use. They are stored away and no longer needed. Hit the delete button on those old thoughts! It was a pivotal moment for me, as I began to take those words to heart. Your heart is the wellspring of life; God's Word teaches us to guard our heart! You might be wondering how to guard your heart. The best way is to be mindful about what you allow in. It's like a garden you water—by daily watering it with the Word of God, you help it grow. The Word of God has the power to transform you, my friend.

I'd like to share something with you that will support your journey to wholeness and help you avoid potential pitfalls. Remember, the enemy has been plotting against you since the day you were born. It wasn't that past relationship that nearly destroyed you or the job you lost. It wasn't a decision you made without thinking it through. It's not even the person who hurt you; it's what the enemy of our souls wants you to believe. No, it goes back to the day you were born. He began scheming then, trying to hold you captive, planting lies in your soul, and making you drag around a backpack filled with giants. For as long as you let him, the enemy will keep executing this plan. Remember, we entered this world as sinners, not yet regenerated in our spirit, so we're like dead men until the Son of God, the Spirit of the Living God, comes to dwell within us. When you pray and cry out for help, God will step in. He's waiting at the door. The enemy came after Jesus in the wilderness, and he will come after every child of God. The good news for you, my friend, is that when you invite Jesus into your heart to take up residence, you gain power over the enemy. You'll be able to slay any giant that taunts you. He's the one who shakes the dry bones and says to you, "Live!" You will witness God bring down your enemies right before your eyes! You now see through a new lens; your sight is adjusted! Wow! What a revelation when this happens in your life.

When it happened to me, I started to dance! I'm lighter on my feet and joy wells up within me now because my gaze is heavenward! It reminds me again that there is nothing more beautiful than seeing a couple on the dance floor. He leads, and she follows. Nothing is more beautiful!

Have you ever been so caught up in a moment that you struggle to enjoy it? Your mind is trying to figure it out. You may be trying to enjoy the experience, but you're distracted by analyzing how you got there and what the purpose is. Down the rabbit hole you go! That little hamster on the wheel is running fast. I began this chapter by talking about new shoes. Let me connect the dots. As I was praying, God began to speak to me about new shoes—not the kind you get in the mail. There is divine direction in His message about new shoes. When I realized He had new shoes in mind for the title of this chapter, I knew He was talking to me about direction. Shoes take us places. So, when we are in a new chapter of our lives and can't see what's ahead, our first reaction is usually fear. We're afraid of the unknown and the adventure, if we're honest. I began questioning the Father about this new chapter. Why new shoes, Jesus? What's going to happen next? What's around the corner? Is change coming, Lord? What's wrong with the old ones? Well, if you've walked with Jesus for any length of time, you learn that there's nothing to fear but fear itself. You also learn that He doesn't answer every question when you ask it, but He will eventually.

I remember my mother telling me about her childhood and how they grew up poor. When she got a new pair of shoes, it was a very special day. She only got one new pair each year, and if it were a tough financial year, she would just inherit her sister's old ones. Growing up in a home with nine children, we usually just received hand-me-downs. So, when my mother did get a new pair of shoes, it was a real treat.

As I walk with my Father, I notice how He does things and find this to be true. Don't miss this! I am learning that if I experience something in my spirit, I will usually experience it physically as well. Let me give you an example. Let's turn to the Word of God. In John 4, (my paraphrasing) Jesus was sitting at the well when a Samaritan woman walked up, and Jesus asked her for a drink of water. In those days, it wasn't kosher for a Jew to even be around a Samaritan, much less ask for anything, but

Jesus was reaching out to this woman because He knew her. He knew she needed something from Him. So, He asked her for a drink of water. This was her invitation—a chance for her to come to Him! She was completely surprised that He was talking to her, and she questioned why He would ask her for anything. Jesus told her that if she knew who was asking her for water, she would ask Him for water, and He would give her living water so she would never thirst again. The Samaritan woman responded, "Sir, give me this water, so I will never thirst again." He was pursuing her, but do you see how He used physical water to speak to her about spiritual things? It is water that gives life to everything. We need water to live! We need Jesus to live, too! He came to her at the well because He knew she needed living water. It all started with a drink of water from the well.

So here I am, after a storm entered my life, sitting in the middle of it, and I too needed something from Jesus. One evening, I went for a walk in my neighborhood. Remember, Jesus is pursuing you and me, and if we listen and look for Him, we won't be disappointed. I did my usual walk, about a mile and a half around my neighborhood, and was about to turn down my street to go home when I felt the nudge of the Holy Spirit urging me to keep walking down this street instead of making the turn. I thought, why not? It's not like the Hallmark channel and the couch won't be there when I get home; they can wait a few more minutes. I kept walking to the next street, and as I passed by a house, I noticed a sign in the yard. I caught a glimpse of one of the words on it, and it caught my attention.

I moved closer. When I saw what it said, I knew it was straight from the throne room. My heart was thrilled! As I mentioned earlier, God doesn't always answer your prayers immediately, but He will eventually. The sign in the yard read, "New Beginnings Construction." New beginnings! That was exactly where I was, and new beginnings can be scary because they also mean something is ending. God knows when we're scared.

As I stood in front of the house that was under construction, I saw firsthand what construction looked like. It's messy and a place where you wouldn't want your kids to play. It screams danger! Standing in front of this construction site, I saw a resemblance to my own house and life. I began to understand some things. New Beginnings Construction Company was about to give this old house a resurrection. God speaks, just when you need it, and in a way that you can understand. My revelations were coming! New shoes meant new beginnings! He had done it again! Tears welled up and streamed down my face. He needed me to see this sign so I would know He is up to something new and good in my life. He doesn't tear down without rebuilding, and He wanted to reassure me that new construction is taking place even if I can't see it. My heart began to settle down in my chest. My heartbeat returned to its normal rhythm. He had spoken! He had confirmed and reassured me that evening. The fear of the unknown dissipated into thin air, and I was comforted by His peace. It isn't easy when God comes in and cleans out the clutter in our lives. Look at how Jesus walked into the temple and was furious at what was happening there. God's temple a marketplace? I don't think so! It is "Holy Business" what He does in our lives. I am sure you understand why the sign 'New Beginnings Construction' was a comfort to me. I walked away smiling, raising my eyes toward heaven and thanking Him all the way home.

The next day, as I woke up, it hit me that I had just ordered a new pair of shoes, and they were set to be delivered that day. The irony made me smile. He showed me once again that His timing is always perfect. New shoes symbolize new beginnings! Many things have changed in my life, and more changes are on the way. I knew this. I can honestly say that His grace has carried me this far, and although I was still in the dark about what the days ahead hold, I knew God was ahead of me, lighting my path.

After 25 years in the house where I was married and raised our four boys, my address will eventually change. Things can change, and they can change suddenly, but one thing will not change—His Word is constant! He is an unchanging God! Psalm 138:8 declares, "The Lord will fulfill his purpose for me." We have God with us, and He will see us through. The new shoes I ordered will arrive today. There are no coincidences with God; He's right on time. He speaks first, then He confirms His Word! I desire more than anything to dance with Jesus, and I can't wait to put on my new spiritual shoes. I am excited to see what He has in store for me!

***

Transformation of Our Mind

I was battered, but not broken,

I was beaten, but not done.

I was bruised, but not shattered,

I fell, but was not down.

I was ill-treated, but not sick,

I was stirred, but not moved.

I was whipped, but I still remain whole through His Grace.

I now have Peace and not envy,

I am filled with Love and not hate.

I am full of Joy and not sorrow,

I have become satisfied with no regrets.

I now show kindness and mercy with patience from the Father.

How did I get from there to here?

I kept Jesus close and near.

How to get from here to there?

Start with a little step from nowhere to big steps to somewhere.

The Focus Goal is Jesus.

Aim high because when you look up at the sky there is no end.

So, Aim high with Expectation........He has Risen!!!!

~ Meaca Rochelle

Salty Coffee

R ecently, I woke up early, not feeling myself. Emotions and stressful situations have a way of doing that to us. As I got up, I knew there was only one place for me to go. It would be another one of those mornings where I would always go and lay out my fluffy white blanket on the carpet beside the French doors, allowing me to look up towards heaven. It was the place where I met with God.

This day felt unusually heavy. I started making coffee, barely able to see because my eyes weren't even awake yet. It was still dark outside. My body was just going through the motions. I laid out my fluffy white blanket on the floor and went back to the kitchen to get my coffee. I could feel tears building up. I knew I needed to pray. Honestly, I've cried a lot through all the changes in my life. One can only cry so much, right? Maybe you can relate. Maybe you've been in a similar place. I had a lot on my mind. Many questions with answers—yes, answers—but even when you find answers, sometimes you still have questions. Can you relate to that? It's like you can't move past one of those "sudden" moments in your life. You're trying to wrap your head around it. I truly understood it, yet I still struggled.

It takes a heart yielded to Christ to be brave enough to let the answers to the questions you've asked sink in and accept the reality of the situation. On this day, I just needed to sit with my Father, and He was calling me. You see, He was waking me up and leading me to my fluffy white blanket under the big sky, and I didn't even realize it. He had something He wanted to tell me. He knows our thoughts, and He knew I had other things on my mind, like what direction my book was going; I needed His inspiration. He knows our thoughts, my friend.

With my coffee in hand, I walked over to my fluffy blanket. I leaned down to touch the floor with one hand, and at the same time, I took a sip of coffee with my other hand. You will never guess what collided. I had the strangest taste in my mouth. In that moment, it occurred to me that I had just tasted coffee for the first time, intermingled with a big tear that rolled down my cheek and slipped into the rim of my coffee mug. It was a moment! One I will never forget. As I was trying to figure out this taste in my mouth, I heard a gentle whisper, "Salty coffee." Immediately, I knew God was giving me guidance for this chapter of the book.

I began to pray, waiting for guidance, and God answered. At first, I just sobbed. I love it when God speaks! I knew as soon as I heard those words that it would be the start of a new chapter.

I simply looked up into the heavens as I absorbed the moment and realized how closely connected He is to His children. He had seen my tears and knew I was concerned about the crying, wondering if the tears would ever stop. God found me that day and invited me to sit with Him so He could speak to me.

After a few minutes of weeping, I collected my emotions and asked God another question. "Lord, what about all these tears?" He already knew the answer. He reminded me of Mary Magdalene. The story is in Luke, Chapter 7, and it describes a troubled woman who met Jesus. She was brave as she entered the home of a Pharisee and made her way past the crowd in the room to sit at Jesus' feet, where she began to weep. As she sat weeping at His feet, she took her hair and dried the tears on His feet. You know, Jesus didn't stop her. It was an act of love she was showing, and as Simon and the others watched, they wondered in their hearts if Jesus knew this woman and her reputation. Jesus knew their thoughts and began to tell them that He knew this woman and who she was. In the same breath, He said she loved much because she had been forgiven much. On the other hand, they hadn't even prepared a place for Him when He came into their home, nor had anyone washed His feet upon entering. His message to them was that those who are forgiven much also love much; Jesus had forgiven her.[1]

As I pondered this demonstration of love, lying on the floor in my tears, I began to see. That story of Jesus' compassion for Mary reminded me that there is beauty in being broken and letting Jesus into our hearts. He immediately reminded me that those who sow in tears will reap with songs of joy. Oh! To be filled with joy! I realized at that moment that I shouldn't worry about all the crying. My tears weren't wasted, and I also knew that my tears weren't only from brokenness, but like Mary, my tears came from seeing His love for me. Tears of loss, tears of broken dreams, tears of grief, but also tears of joy from feeling so much love as I have witnessed His care for me, guiding my steps daily. Seeing His hand of protection around me, just as He protected Mary, the only one who washed His feet that day.

Jesus stepped up and covered Mary that day in the house filled with disciples and Pharisees who were judging her and Jesus' response to her because of her broken past. He loved her and affirmed her.[2] My tears will no longer concern me. God reminded me of the law of sowing and reaping that morning. I will sow!

During the days that followed, I started studying scripture about the law of sowing and reaping. If I am sowing, then I need to understand the reaping. The first verse I found, which is probably my favorite, is Psalm 126:5-6: "Those who sow in tears will reap in songs of joy. He who goes out weeping, carrying seed to sow, will return with songs of joy, carrying sheaves with him." They would come back singing songs of joy and carrying sheaves of grain, which was their harvest. That morning, as I sipped salty coffee, he reminded me of this verse. Psalm 30:5 says, "For His anger is but for a moment, and his favor is for a lifetime. Weeping may tarry for the night, but joy comes in the morning."

Amid all this, I felt like a jigsaw puzzle with a missing piece. Joy was the piece I was searching for because, through all the tears, it was hard to find. We've all experienced broken promises and broken hearts. Brokenness can lead to terrible things happening. It makes us stop taking the word 'promise' seriously. I don't think any of us mean to do that, but when life disappoints, it can happen.

My friend, I have good news! There is one that will remain, and His name is Jesus. I have come to remind you that He is a promise keeper. You can stand on God's Word; it is true, and you should never doubt. Galatians 6:9 has a promise, and it says, "Let us not be weary in doing good, for at the proper time we will reap a harvest if we do not give up." I love the part, "we will reap a harvest"—there's nothing to misunderstand about that verse. I continued seeking in the scripture and I found more. Hebrews 12:2 was very helpful. Jesus exemplifies just how we are to live. "Looking to Jesus, the founder, and perfecter of our faith, who for the joy that was set before Him endured the cross, despising the shame, and is seated at the right hand of the throne of God." He looked past the cross and kept his eyes on where He was going. This would pass, and He knew it; the future was what He stayed focused on.

Jesus said, "The thief does not come except to steal, and to kill, and to destroy. I have come that they may have life, and that they may have it more abundantly."[3] The beautiful part of the love story I shared in my first book, The Invitation, is that He truly will come for you. He saw me and made a way for me. He invited me to come out into the deep and walk with Him. He wanted to give me life! "For to the one who pleases him God has given wisdom and knowledge and joy, but to the sinner he has given the business of gathering and collecting, only to give to the one who pleases God."[4]

I want nothing more than to please Jesus! Listen, my friend — Jeremiah, known as the weeping prophet, said, "Your words were found, and I ate them, and your words became to me a joy and the delight of my heart, for I am called by your name, O Lord, God of hosts."[5] That's how we stand on His Word, my friend — we read it, and we consume it into our inner parts. Reading the Bible can be intimidating for some, but I encourage you to try it. It's called the Living Word, and it will speak to you and your situation. There was a time in my life when I didn't have a strong desire to read the Bible. Today, my prayer is that God will make me hungry for His Word. Jesus loves a prayer like that! Just being open and pouring out our hearts to Him is what it's all about, my friend. We come just as we are! It's a relationship with your Creator that He wants to have with you — a beautiful, loving relationship.

Another prophet I looked to for guidance was Isaiah. In Chapter 61 of Isaiah, I found comfort in these words: "He will comfort all who mourn and provide for those who grieve in Zion; to bestow on them a crown of beauty instead of ashes, the oil of gladness instead of mourning, and a garment of praise instead of a spirit of despair."[6] Isaiah ministered to the children of God, giving them hope in these verses, which still apply to us today.

I took these scriptures and more, posted them all around my house, and kept them before me so I wouldn't forget His promises. I was seeking joy and gladness—not the simple kind that comes from going to the store and buying myself something pretty. That kind of joy is only temporary. I was after the kind of joy and gladness that are deep inside our souls, and no one can take that away from us. As the days went by, I continued to meet my Father down on the floor in front of the big sky.

You have probably heard the saying "When it rains, it pours." During those days of trying to persevere, I was working with preschool children, and I got Covid. One of my little ones at school had it, and I was sick the very next day. I went down with the worst headache, a fever, and was quarantined in my bedroom. Two of my sons were visiting from Nashville, and I didn't want to pass it on to them. I was grateful they were home because they took care of me and visited me at the doorway of my room. By day four, I was not improving. I still felt terrible, still had a fever, and I was starting to sink into the abyss. I wondered if I would ever feel normal again.

I'm convalescing in my bed, and my bedroom looks like the Garden of Eden. There is a lot of time to sit and think while we lie in bed sick, but this might work to my advantage. Yes, remember the vision of creating the Garden of Eden in my bedroom? Vision is essential, my friend! Quarantined in the Garden of Eden was good for me, and I stayed long enough for God to show me a few things. On day five, my eyes open, and I think I might be feeling like my old self again. I didn't move; I just kept lying on my pillow and evaluating the situation. Thankfully, my conclusion didn't change. I continued to believe I was feeling like my old self again, and I might be getting better. I slowly raised myself out of bed. I actually desired a cup of coffee and tiptoed downstairs to make it. I stopped to read my little devotion for that day that was set on my kitchen counter; it couldn't have been more timely.

I read about how David was anointed King by Samuel, the prophet, while he was still young, but he went through many trials before becoming King of Jerusalem. He had much to learn from God about trusting Him in every situation and then letting God guide him through it, so he could become the compassionate leader God intended him to be for His people. I sat there smiling to myself. All the questions I had just didn't seem as important anymore. If David could face trials and learn to trust God in tough times, then I can, too.

I made my coffee and was walking back upstairs when God directed my attention to one of my favorite books by A.W. Tozer, *The Pursuit of God*.[7] I knew there was something He wanted me to see. So, I picked it up and headed back to my room. I got comfortable in my bed; I was truly feeling so much better. I opened my book to see what God wanted to show me. My bookmark was at the chapter titled "The Universal Presence," and I began reading. I started to sit up and pay close attention when I read about the Patriarch Jacob, in Genesis 28:16. "Surely the Lord is in this place, and I knew it not." Jacob was also questioning whether God was present at that time in his life. He was in trouble with his brother and had to flee for his life. In a dream, the Lord spoke to him and gave him direction, and as he awoke, he realized that God was there all the time, but he hadn't known it. I believe we all struggle with that one from time to time. It was in that moment that I came to realize God had been with me all my life. God was there from the beginning— not only walking alongside me but sometimes carrying me when I could not carry myself. Oh, relief had come! God had spoken to me today, carrying me back to my childhood and reassuring me that He was there. Thinking God isn't there in the worst of times is our greatest downfall and simply a lie the enemy wants you to believe.

On my bed of affliction, God showed me He was always there. Something else happened that morning: I felt joy returning. He was with me! Yes, I realized something very important: joy, real joy, is knowing that the Father has you in His hands and He is guiding us even when we don't see or feel anything. If Jacob can miss it, we can too! In the span of a day, I was on the brink of the abyss, feeling down and discouraged, but Joy comes in the morning, and God showed up, reminding me that through all the trials, I can count on Him. I can count on Him in sickness, heartbreak, loss, and looking back throughout my life. I see the work of His hands in every hardship. He knows the end from the beginning of our stories. Trust Him!

I'll leave you with this verse that has become so meaningful to me: "You make known to me the path of life; in your Presence, there is fullness of Joy."[8] In the past, I struggled to understand this verse until the fifth day of my illness. Now I realize that there is always joy in God's Presence; it is there for us to receive. He is in control of our lives. God is with us, and in His presence is true joy. I now believe that He is in control through the good, the bad, and the ugly, and that has made life so much easier for me.

God wants to give us our heart's desire, but we have to give Him the reins. That alone will make you shout all over the house! I shouted all over the house that day, and I also grabbed a can of Lysol to get rid of some germs at the same time. I was happy to have found this missing piece of my puzzle, joy. Honestly, it wasn't missing at all. I just needed to realize it.

Remember this story, and if you are ever on a bed of affliction, look up! He might want to tell you something. No, I don't believe God creates a bed of affliction, not at all. However, the 23rd Psalm does say, "He makes us lie down."[9] I do believe He uses your trials to help you grow in your trust, and He always brings good to your situation. He brings good out of everything!

So, the next time you're sipping a cup of coffee, and your tears turn it into salty coffee, know that for every tear you sow, you will reap a measure of joy. It is God's promise!

Turn North

"I don't think we're in Kansas anymore," said Dorothy to her little dog, Toto. How many of you know where that line comes from? If you've lived a while, you will recognize that line, and for those younger with no idea, I recommend you watch *The Wizard of Oz*.[1] Yes, Dorothy and her little dog, Toto, have just stepped out onto the front porch of her home in the land of Oz. It is a land of brilliant colors and the home of munchkins, good witches, bad witches, and many other interesting things. It is a 1900 fantasy novel written for children by Frank Baum, but it became a movie that captivated audiences worldwide.

The movie begins in Dorothy's small hometown in Kansas, shown in black and white until a tornado hits the area, causing everyone to scramble for safety. Dorothy is nowhere to be found, so when she finally gets home and finds no one there, she runs into the house. She gets hit in the head by an object and blacks out. The story then continues as she is dreaming. In her dream, the house is caught in a twister, and when it lands, she wakes up. As she walks out the door, she finds herself in a different world. "The land of Oz!" It's a land full of bright colors, and she is greeted by the good witch, Glenda, the Witch of the North. Dorothy is amazed. Keep in mind, she's a farm girl from Kansas and hasn't gone far from her own backyard. She's captivated by everything she sees. I remember being captivated, just sitting in front of my TV the first time I watched the movie. She grabs her little dog, holds him close, and steps onto the yellow brick road. She has many questions! Glenda, the good witch, shows her the way. All the munchkins come out and do the same. It's the yellow brick road that will lead her now! Stay tuned; we'll revisit this story.

It all began with a prayer. I was asking God for a Word to stand on! It had to be scripture because only His Word can keep us steady when storms enter our lives. You might say scripture is our yellow brick road. Without the Word of God to stand on during a storm, we too will feel like we've been caught up in a twister — a whirlwind of a different kind. Lies, doubt, unbelief, confusion, chaos—these are the opinions of yourself that form in your mind and overwhelm you. I was praying because I needed a Word. That same evening, late in the day, my friend Doris called. Her calls are always timely. You have to understand that God sends us exactly what we need. Doris was someone who was part of my life while I was growing up. She was my Sunday school teacher when I was a young girl. I knew she cared for me. Some people are sent by God and leave a mark on our lives; she left her mark on my heart. She made me feel special. Decades later, she re-entered my life during the passing of my parents. Day after day, during that time, she was there, waiting if I needed her. I knew I could share my most private thoughts with her, and I trusted her to keep them confidential. My precious mother was always the one I could turn to and share my deepest concerns with, knowing she would never say a word to anyone except God.

Do you see the loving Father and how He meets our needs? He knew exactly how my story would unfold. It was destined for me to reconnect with Doris, someone from my past who held a special place in my heart. Only our Heavenly Father can make that happen! So, the same day I asked for a word to stand on, Doris called me that evening. Her exact words were, "You have been on my heart all day, and I couldn't go to bed until I talked to you and made sure you were alright." Let me tell you, when you are feeling alone and your parents are no longer here on this earth, a phone call like that feels like a call from Heaven. I sat there in awe. I knew her call was perfectly timed. I began to pour out my heart to her and told her about the prayer I had prayed that morning, asking God for a scripture. She said, "Lori, I have the Scripture for you." Doris is a woman of God, and she loves His Word. I knew this was a divine moment. She began to quote scripture to me: "You have been wandering around this hill long enough; now turn north."[2] She continued with another scripture, Moses speaking to God's people: "Do not be afraid; stand firm and you will see the deliverance the Lord will bring you today. The Egyptians you see today, you will never see again. The Lord will fight for you; you need only be still."[3]

Well, how is that for an answered prayer? My heart was touched! I wept. As warm tears streamed down my face, I felt the Lord washing away my troubles. I received this word: "It's time to turn North!" The scripture from Doris was spot on! I had been circling that mountain long enough. Around and around we go, knowing we need a change. We just aren't brave enough yet to leave that path. Sometimes, we don't even realize we are doing this. It is the Lord who speaks to us, through His Word and sometimes through His servants. Our mindsets need a complete overhaul, and sometimes we need a Moses in our lives to help us. Thank God for Doris!

I placed that scripture in my kitchen window where I could see and read it every day. It was uplifting. I knew I was done going around this mountain, and I was ready to dance in my new pair of shoes.

A few weeks went by, and one morning I woke up, grabbed my coffee, and started to pray. I hit the floor where I usually meet Him, and as I was praying, I began to see glimpses of my future. God was showing me highlights of what lay ahead! I thought to myself, "I truly am going North!" Why do I know that? It's just like traveling in a car. Depending on which way you go, that's your scenery too.

We all love traveling to the mountains or the coast. We can't wait to catch our first glimpse of a mountaintop or the shoreline. You know you're getting close by the color of the sand along the side of the road. Our eyes quickly notice the scenery change. I began to see the signs of change as I lay there that morning. It's the little glimpses in the Spirit that He shows you. Yes, God will do that. He will reveal secrets we long to know and offer us glimpses of the future when we are ready. For example, let's look at Moses in the book of Exodus. God gave Moses the command to go to Pharaoh and tell him to let His people go; He also told Moses that Pharaoh would harden his heart and refuse. God told Moses, "Then say to Pharaoh, This is what the Lord says: Israel is my firstborn son, and I told you, "Let my son go, that he may worship me.' But you refused to let him go; so, I will kill your firstborn son."[4] God let Moses know the plan in advance and how it would end. Sometimes we don't see the whole plan, but He is kind enough to give us glimpses!

As I stepped out in faith with my new shoes, He was already going ahead of me. As I turn north, I will encounter new places and scenery. You know, twisters in the Midwest can appear out of nowhere, and life can be the same way. A twister can destroy something you've worked hard to build; storms bring devastation, but we can't just stop and give up. No! We might get knocked around and need a moment to regroup, but like Nehemiah in the Bible, we will rebuild![5] What if there are views and colors you've never seen before? What if the yellow brick road starts the moment you're willing to follow Him? Hope, love, and courage will be right there with you on the way, and He will make sure you meet all three!

Consider Dorothy in The Wizard of Oz; she is on a new journey. As she traveled down that yellow brick road, she met three amazing characters as well. She learned valuable lessons from the Scarecrow; he was the embodiment of hope. I love the Scarecrow. Everyone loves the Scarecrow. The Tin Man has a kind heart; he just doesn't realize it. He showed love to Dorothy when he saw she was frightened. The Cowardly Lion, the last character Dorothy meets, teaches her about courage, but it comes after she gives him a piece of her mind. I think we can all relate to that lion. I know I am using my imagination to inspire you, but I need you to know that He will send those special ones to you when you need help. In the movie, Dorothy had a vision: to get home. Her friends encouraged her and never left her side until she returned home. What I'm trying to say is, you need vision!

Proverbs 29:18 declares, "Where there is no vision, the people perish." This is what King Solomon tells us, and he was known as the wisest man who ever lived. Hosea 4:6 is also about vision. "My people are destroyed from a lack of knowledge." We are destroyed because we do not know what the Word of God says; if we do know, we would be wise to follow it. Turning North is about vision. We need to keep it at the forefront of our minds and display it on the walls of our homes.

A vision board is something I discovered. I created one and displayed it in my home. The reminders on the board keep me focused. I like to think of it as a map. The desires of my heart are posted there. Habakkuk 2:2 says, "And the Lord answered me: Write the vision and make it plain on tablets, that he who reads it may run. For still the vision awaits its appointed time; it hastens to the end - it will not lie. If it seems slow, wait for it; it will surely come; it will not delay." Wow! That is His promise to you. You write your vision down and at the appointed time, it will come to pass. Whatever you sense in your heart, whatever you see in your future is vision. What makes you come alive? What is your deepest desire? That is a vision of your future!

I love this quote by Howard Thurman. "Don't ask what the world needs. Ask what makes you come alive and go do it. Because what the world needs is people who have come alive."[6] Everyone can take some advice from that! We need people who are alive. Full of passion! Your vision board should be filled with things that make you smile, move you to tears, and words written from the deepest trenches of your heart. Pictures! Words! Declarations! That vision board should be as unique as you are.

Why should you write down your vision? Clarity comes when we put it on paper. Writing things down is like a camera zooming in on its subject. I have seen many answered prayers from my vision board. As I watch God move and bring my visions to pass, I note the date when God answered my prayer. Great reminders for us to look back and see what God has done! Share with your children and encourage them to start a vision board. Imagine their faith growing as they see God bringing about things for them at a young age. Picture how it will transform their view of the future. The seeds of faith you plant in their hearts—you will always remember it, and they will never forget it!

It's a new path I am on; I have turned North. It reminds me of something I do when I ride my horse. It is something they teach you when you are riding. When you are riding and want to change direction, let's say you are going to turn in a circle, you should already be looking that way. Yes, when steering anything and you want to go in another direction, you need to start looking that way before it happens. That is a good reminder for you and me, right?

What are you focusing on? Is the path you're on currently serving you in the best way? Do you need to turn north? Do you need to change direction because you're just going around a mountain with no clear destination? Make the decision and turn. You may not find a yellow brick road, but trust God. God has blessings for you, and He will help you find your vision. Make the vision board! Look for the glimpses God will show you, don't be afraid to step out. I want you to experience all God has for you. Be brave.

The Unveiling

One day, I heard the Lord speak the word "unveiling" to me. I knew I didn't think this word up myself, so I knew the Holy Spirit was speaking to me. I had an idea of what the word meant, but I didn't want to miss anything, so I googled it and found several definitions. These included the removal of a veil, presenting something in public for the first time, and, in a biblical sense, unveiling as a revelation. The word "revelation" means the pulling back of the veil, so we can see what was hidden from us before. All of these meanings intrigued me, and I was on a quest to discover what might be hidden. What truths is God trying to reveal to me?

When I first heard that word, my mind quickly imagined an art gallery and the unveiling of a masterpiece. It reminded me of an artist's work—sculpting and creating in hopes of sharing it with the world. Just like a composer crafts a song, an artist of a different kind creates something new from nothing—a marvelous wonder. God is behind all creativity. I believe that all inspiration begins with God.

I also thought about the unveiling of a bride. It is the most important day in a woman's life. She will prepare herself for her husband, and the veil will be lifted when he sees his bride for the first time that day. This is truly an unveiling, and the marriage is blessed by God.

In Genesis, you can read about the first unveiling. It was a divine moment in the Garden of Eden—perhaps you know the story of what God did in the beginning. In six days, He created everything, then He rested. He spoke things into existence, and it was good. The last thing He created was a companion for Adam. God said, "It was not good for man to be alone, and so I will make a helper suitable for him." In the second chapter of Genesis, God explains how He made the woman. He caused Adam to fall into a deep sleep, and while he was sleeping, He took a rib from Adam's side to make the woman. As Adam slept, the Lord God, in all His creativity, made a woman and brought her to Adam. Yes, that was truly the first unveiling—He brought her to Adam! You can see how she would complete him; she came from his side. When a man loves and cares for his wife deeply, he loves and cares for himself. She would come alongside him as his helper. When she loves and cares for him, she also loves and cares for herself. They become one. It's still amazing to see how God brings together a man and a woman. You can understand why the Father wants to be right in the center of this union. It's His creation, with love, peace, and glory as its ingredients. When the Father created that moment in the Garden of Eden, this was Adam's response: "This is now bone of my bones and flesh of my flesh; she shall be called woman. She was taken out of man."[1]

An earthly father has the honor of walking his daughter down the aisle and giving her away to the person she has chosen to spend forever with. In some cases, when the father is not present, we know someone special steps into that role. What an incredible privilege it is to walk her down the aisle and give her away to the one she will be betrothed. It is a Garden of Eden experience each time. For the bride, two of the most important men in her life will be her father and her husband. For every woman, the question since the day she was born is "Am I lovely?" It's a question her father has hopefully answered, and on that special day, when she sees her husband, that's all she wants to hear. "Am I lovely to you?"

On the other hand, guys have a different question, but just as important. They want to know "Do I have what it takes?" The book, *Captivating*, is a must-read![2] It is written by John and Stasi Eldredge, and they uncovered so much to help me understand about the character of a man and a woman. These two questions we each have seem easy to answer, but if left unanswered, they can cause a lot of heartache and self-doubt in our lives.

Since reading the book, *Captivating*, I have been thinking about the question, "Am I lovely?" If her father doesn't answer that question, then sadly, a young girl grows up still needing that question answered. What does she do? Sometimes, and most of the time, she looks in the mirror, and this is where the enemy begins to work to destroy the masterpiece that God has created. Ephesians 2:10 says, "For we are God's masterpiece. He has created us anew in Christ Jesus, so we can do the good things he planned for us long ago." We have within us a beauty much more profound and deeper than what the mirror shows us, and God wants to remove the veil from our hearts. We will discover our true value if we examine the Word of God and believe what God says about us. The mirror of the Word of God speaks truth to us.

Since we're talking about beauty, let's think about our hearts for a moment. We are taught through scripture, "As a man thinketh in his heart, so is he!"[3] Another verse about the heart says, "Above all else, guard your heart, because it is the wellspring of life."[4] It's interesting—God says our heart is the wellspring of life. Please pause and reflect on this. King Solomon advises us to guard it because it is the source of everything else in our lives. In short, a wellspring is a stream that flows outward, so whatever enters the heart will eventually flow out. Even after this revelation, I had more questions. First, why do people place so much importance on their outward appearance? Why is the mirror such a powerful symbol? And what about our hearts? Does inward beauty shine through? After prayer and reflection, I concluded that our heart is our greatest asset. Instead of seeking approval for our physical beauty, we should focus on inner beauty—the beauty of the heart. It would make life much easier for everyone. For me, the question "Am I lovely?" was just too loud in my mind. I longed for my dad to answer that question. Oh, how I adored him and yearned for a close relationship with him.

I am turning 59 years old tomorrow, and now the truth has never been clearer. You could say I had an unveiling. A revelation! The Lord took me to His Word, and I found answers in Exodus 34:29-35. He showed me what can happen when our hearts live in God's presence. Moses had been with God for forty days on Mount Sinai, receiving instructions to lead the people of Israel successfully. When he came down from the mountain with the two tablets, the Ten Commandments, he was unaware that his face was radiant because he had been in God's presence. Aaron and the Israelites saw him and were afraid to come near. He called to them, and the congregation gathered. Because of his radiant face, a veil was placed over his face while he spoke to them. Consider this: if Moses's face was radiant with the Old Covenant, which was passing away soon, how much greater is the glory of the New Covenant? 2 Corinthians 3:16-18 says, "But whenever anyone turns to the Lord, the veil is taken away. Now the Lord is the Spirit, and where the Spirit of the Lord is, there is freedom. And we, who with unveiled faces all reflect the Lord's glory, are being transformed into His likeness with ever-increasing glory, which comes from the Lord." This is the unveiling I believe God wanted me to see. With our unveiled faces, we reflect the Lord's glory! When we turn to Him, the veil is removed! We will see Him in our lives, and we will notice transformation beginning. We are being transformed into His likeness, which comes from the Lord. Our heart is where beauty begins, but only as we turn to the Lord.

I would like to share an excerpt from *The Pursuit of God* by A.W. Tozer. He discusses our inner life and the veil in our hearts. "Self is the opaque veil in our heart and how this veil hides the face of God from us."[5] It is not a veil that we can remove, but we must invite God to do the work in our hearts. It is never easy to tear through the tender layers life has shaped us with, and it can be painful, just as the cross was a painful experience for Jesus. However, it was what the cross did to Jesus and what it will do to every man that will set him free. It is a work of God in us and a work only He can perform. Our role is to invite Him, and to yield! Just as we read in Corinthians, when we turn to the Lord, the veil is taken away. Our surrender to Him, just as Jesus surrendered to the Father, will bring resurrection, glory, and power. For joy, the veil is taken away. The veil is removed, and we see Him face-to-face. As we yield and remain in faith, we will see that God is doing something!

During this season of my life, I found comfort in Psalm 121. "I lift my eyes to the hills - where does my help come from? My help comes from the Lord, the Maker of heaven and ear th."[6] I knew God was removing a veil from my heart, and it was painful. This morning, as I was having coffee and walking through the house, I passed by an antique piece of furniture that holds many things dear to me. As I walked past, I felt a check in my Spirit to stop and look through these belongings.

When I reached the bottom shelf, I saw my mom's Bible, and on top of it lay the shofar that she held very dear. When she needed help, I remember her telling me how she would blow the shofar, an instrument used in the Old Testament. Israel would blow the shofar when they needed God to come through for them. Essentially, they were asking for help when they blew the shofar.[7] She believed it was an act of faith, and God would answer.

Well, here I was, needing God's help. I was hurting. Life was painful, and I faced two choices at that moment. Would I brush it off and lay it back on her Bible, or would I blow the shofar? I had forgotten about the shofar because it was tucked away on a shelf. I knew exactly what to do! I blew that shofar, and I knew God heard me and saw my faith. I put it back where it belonged, thinking, I hope my mom heard it too. I started to feel the struggle lift. I called on Him, knowing He would help me. Sometimes we get stuck, life gets hard, and we need the Father's help. After that day, He began to reveal some things to me. He showed me the healing happening in my life. He was removing the veil from my heart so I could see Him face to face.

That's why we are here. Our hearts are connected to God's heart and everything around us. I came across a beautiful quote that I believe we should meditate on: "We are not human beings having a spiritual experience, we are spiritual beings having a human experience," profound words by Pierre Teilhard de Chardin.[8]

The mystery of God, the bride of Christ, resembles a bride on her wedding day. She wants to be perfect. On that special day, she brings a glimpse of her beauty embodied in lace and a heart full of love. The veil she wears will be lifted by her husband. The same applies to you and me. We are the bride of Christ, and we bring glory to Him as we prepare ourselves for our bridegroom.

My son Blake just released a song called "Pretty Face."[9] It is one of my favorite songs because it describes a girl. However, everything he describes about this girl focuses on her inner qualities. Her beauty comes from within. My favorite line is "She is beautiful, but what makes you stay, she ain't just a pretty face." What a line! It speaks to me every time! I believe God is trying to speak here as well. Beauty is more than skin deep. I believe what our hearts hold inside will show on our faces. "For you created my inmost being, you knit me together in my mother's womb."[10] God took the time to knit us together, and we are made in His image. If we focus on God's word and the importance of our hearts, it can begin our journey of transformation.

The final creation by God, his crown of glory, "woman." She was called Eve, which means life. I'm reminded of a movie I saw, "My Big Fat Greek Wedding," where Tula asks Ian, her fiancé, "Why do you love me?" I sat on the edge of my seat waiting for his answer. Do you know what he said? "Because you have brought life back to me!"[11] Wow, I thought, can a woman do that to someone? If we are joined to the right person, the answer is yes, we can bring life to another. I know we bring life into the world at the birth of our children, and there is no greater joy than experiencing this gift. But can we also bring life to another? Yes, Eve's name means life! She brought life to Adam. We are life-givers to each other, to our children, and to this world. We have it within us, and the enemy knows it! If we allow what the Word of God says about us to sink in and replace the conditioned thoughts we've had about ourselves over the years, it will change our story.

The events that happened to you in this lifetime were not your fault. However, it's easy to take on guilt and shame. Maybe things happened to you repeatedly, causing pain. Remember, the message you received from those experiences can be erased. The enemy planned to destroy the life within you, but Christ has redeemed what was happening in your life. He has made you new. You are still here, but now you belong to Him. You might get stuck, and your wheels might spin like mine, but now you know who to call for help. My precious mother would tell you that blowing the Shofar is not a bad idea either!

As I near the conclusion of *Dancing with Jesus*, I was reminded this morning of the message in Psalm 139. My mother wrote me many letters during her life, and in every letter, beside her name, was Psalm 139. It is also highlighted in my Bible. As I read that Psalm today, I reached the last two verses: "Search me, O God, and know my heart; test me and know my anxious thoughts. See if there is any hurtful way in me and lead me in the way everlasting." I prayed, and as tears welled up, I knew I needed God's help again. I wanted to understand my heart better. I wanted Him to show me any hurtful ways in my heart that I couldn't see. I wanted Him to lift that veil if anything was hidden there, preventing me from a closer relationship with Him. God was taking care of Holy business right there with me.

My journey has been challenging, and I can tell you that even change for your good is not always easy. Know this: God's grace will be there. His help will arrive exactly when needed. I am excited because I have never been this girl before. That's right, God is revealing me, not in an art gallery, but on a much grander scale, to a world that needs hope. His purpose is to give life to all, and His delight is to do so through me. I am His Masterpiece.

As Moses didn't realize His face shone with the Glory of God after being with Him for forty days on a mountain, I have also come to realize some things. First and foremost, dancing with Jesus was the most important decision I ever made. Second, Jesus is gentle, and He loves me. Third, He never gives up on His children. Lastly, He came to set us free. We don't need to hide from God! We need to hide in God!

God may want to lift the veil from your heart, and if so, trust Him. There is nothing to do but surrender yourself to Him. When the cross has done its work, you will be able to say, I am free, I am loved, and you will realize it all came from the gentle hands of Almighty God. To see Him face to face and know you are His will be worth it all. He is shaping in you a masterpiece to reveal to the world. The masterpiece is YOU!

My Dance

A s I wrap up *Dancing with Jesus*, I want to share my dance and the miracle God preserved for me. Our Father desires an intimate relationship with us, and I believe that's why He chose the word "dancing" when communicating with me. It is a joyful word, and joy always invites us to communion with Him.

Nine years ago, I stood on the shores of Topsail, trying to hold myself together from all the wreckage that had recently occurred. I believe that moment was a divine appointment with God. At the lowest point in my life, He saw me. On the shoreline of Topsail, staring out into the deep water, He invited me to come out to the deep with Him. It was the hardest place I had ever been. He offered me His hand and led me through the sadness, grief, trauma, and loss that the last ten years had brought to me and my family. I felt comforted knowing I was not alone. I sensed His arms around me as I stood on the shore, and I took His hand by faith that day. He is a compassionate

God and loving Father, and He was with me. This was going to be hard, and He knew it.

At some point, I don't know how long it took me, I was walking through so much, but He wanted me to look up. There was a plan in place that I didn't know about. God wanted me to trust Him with it all. I wanted to trust Him. I wanted to believe that all my dreams and desires were still alive somewhere because I felt that I had lost them. I had to believe that He and only He could bring something beautiful out of the wreckage of my life. Unfortunately, I could only see the wreckage, but God wanted me to get a glimpse of the beauty within the brokenness.

There is something beautiful about brokenness. In that vulnerable time, we see the hand of our loving Father pick us up and restore us. Nothing is more beautiful than that! If I could imagine Him and me dancing together as He led me, He knew I could start dreaming again. What a loving Father we have! I hope, as I have shared with you, you will see that He danced me right out of the hardest places I have ever walked. He knew the words to speak to me and the exact timing of when to speak them. God knew the desires of my heart. As we danced through it all, He began to bring life to me; He breathed love and peace into my soul. When we go through hard places in our lives, we think we can never get back up. The devastation is too much. God wants you to know that He is so much bigger than any trial you are going through today.

God also had another dance planned for me. He knew my prayer as a young girl. Every girl dreams of this dance. I dreamed of it! No, I did more than that! I remember standing in the middle of a field as a young girl, looking up into the sky and praying a special prayer to Him. It was the first prayer I remember very clearly. I remember where I was and what I asked. I asked my Father, in faith, if He would someday let me experience love—a love that would be a "happily ever after" love. I wanted to be married to the one person God had for me, and I longed to experience unconditional love between a man and a woman. I believed it could truly exist, and I wanted it. I prayed that prayer when I was young; but now, after all the hurt and heartache I've gone through in life, I was suddenly unsure if it would happen. Our Father is full of surprises and miracles! This is a beautiful love story and undoubtedly a miracle. Some stories are worth telling a million times, and this is one of them. I need to go back a few years to when it all began—35 years ago. Little did I know, God had been working out a plan for me all along! It came as a surprise to me, but God knew from the start.

It all began with my wonderful friend Gail! I met her in my early twenties at work. We quickly became great friends, and as our friendship grew, she started telling me about a young man who was a dear friend of hers and whom she thought we should meet. His name was Kyle. Gail grew up in the same neighborhood as Kyle. Their families were friends and became more like family over the years. She loved Kyle like a brother. She kept talking about him and wanted me to meet him. Eventually, I gathered the courage to do just that. It feels like yesterday, and I still remember the moment. Gail invited Kyle to stop by work one afternoon. It seemed harmless, but I was pretty nervous. When the day finally arrived and I saw him walk through the door, I knew it was him because he just stopped and looked at me. When he stopped, it felt like everything else froze, including my heart. I remember thinking, wow, he is perfect. Then I started hoping it really was Kyle. Moments like this come once in a lifetime, and I was having one. It was Kyle!

Kyle started walking straight toward me. Now I am very sure that my heart began beating again because I could feel it pulsate inside my chest. I must tell you that he wasn't just perfect, but as we stood there talking, I also noticed something else. He was polished, too! I found nothing wrong with him! It's funny now, but it wasn't then, because as I saw, he had it all together, and since you have been reading my book, you know I did not! I am sure part of me thought about grabbing some running shoes and hi-tailing it out of there right then, but my heart was embracing this moment. I was trying so hard to be brave through the nerves. We chatted for a few minutes, and I can't tell you what we said that day. Soon after, we started dating. I remember several dates we had together, and we were having fun. On one of our dates, he took me jogging on a trail in Duke Forest, where he jogged frequently. I jogged very little at that time, but I took him up on it. I probably had shin splints after that run, but I made sure to keep up with him. I also had the privilege of meeting his mom and dad. They were loving parents, and his family was so sweet.

Kyle also took me to lunch one afternoon at the country club where he played golf. I remember that day very well. The tables were decorated with white linen and were beautifully set in a room lined with windows. We ate lunch while overlooking this grand view of a beautiful golf course. That was the day I knew for sure! The day I realized I was in way over my head. I wanted to run! I wanted to stay! Boy, was I scared!

One night, Kyle picked me up, and we went dancing. Yes, dancing! I was thinking about not wanting to dance in front of this guy; I was too shy. He loved to dance, and he invited me to come along. So, I said, sure! I knew that night I would need some liquid courage to pull it off. I had one drink and thought, if one glass of courage is good, then two glasses in, I will be a dancing queen. An hour into the evening, maybe not even that long, I wasn't myself. Kyle noticed it too, and probably wasn't happy about it. Finally, after he found me, he came over and said he was going to leave. He offered to take me home, and the decision I made that night, under the influence of alcohol, was going to cost me. We parted ways that night, and I never saw Kyle again. It was a terrible moment. Miraculously, I did get a ride home, and let's all agree that God truly watches over us! As a Father, He probably thought I deserved a good spanking, too.

I woke up the next morning feeling terrible. Not because of the alcohol, but due to another problem. A problem that wasn't going away anytime soon: I had hurt someone. I couldn't face Kyle; I was too ashamed. I was never able to tell Kyle about the struggles I was going through at that time; I kept it all hidden behind makeup and a smile. Too ashamed to tell anyone, and that was just another mistake that made the giants bigger. So that night at the dance gave me a good reason to run! Run from him and run from all the giants inside that haunted me. Instead of facing them, I chose to put on my running shoes. At least Kyle deserved an apology from me. I am not proud of what I did, and I carried that burden in my heart for thirty-five years. I thought about it from time to time and even told people about this terrible thing I once did to someone very special. I will never forget it.

Fast forward 35 years, and I am sitting alone on my couch. Life can throw you a curveball, and it hits so hard that it knocks you down. I had been knocked down. For a few years, I found myself watching Hallmark movies from the comfort of my couch. I still believed in love, and my dreams hadn't died after all. I still thought about that prayer when I looked into the heavens as a young girl standing in a field. I wanted to live a happily married life and experience true love. God saw me then, and He also saw me on the couch watching Hallmark movies decades later. He saw the tears, the struggles, and the battles I fought for so long. Struggles are painful, and just like a splinter, they need to come out. For two years, God and I worked on that as I sat on the couch. He began to pull out the splinters and heal the pain from my childhood and the sadness life had brought me. He spoke the truth through His Word. Yes, the Word of God changed my way of thinking, and I was healing. Day by day, verse by verse, God's Word began to sink in. It would take some time, but the dreams and desires inside me remained. I believe He placed them there. He still wanted to give me the desires of my heart.

One of those evenings, I was on the couch, just happened to be on Facebook at the right moment while watching a Hallmark movie with my dog Bella lying next to me. I was living my dream through a Hallmark movie; something we might be doing without realizing it. As I looked at my phone, my friend Gail's name popped up. Seeing Gail's name—the friend who introduced me to Kyle years ago—I immediately thought of him. I thought to myself, he was such a kind person. Then I had an even better thought! I could now apologize to him. Yes, I owed this man an apology and an explanation. I might not have been able to face him back then, but God had been doing deep work in my heart, and I was now able to face things rather than run. I reached out to Gail for help with this, but I didn't hear from her. That's when I took matters into my own hands. I wrote Kyle a sincere letter of apology. As I began to write, I thought about what I had done that night and how he had to drive home alone. Oh, my goodness, how that must have felt for him. As I wrote, the words just came—sincere words—and I felt a little better knowing he would receive this letter soon. I knew in my heart that this apology would hopefully help heal some of that awful night for Kyle.

As I reflected on that night 35 years ago, I wanted to explain to Kyle what I was going through back then. I hoped and prayed I would get the chance to do so. In the last two years, God has pulled back the curtain on insecurity, and thankfully so, because the truth is much clearer now. I was also starting to understand what shame does to a person. Shame makes us believe we are flawed, which causes us to want to hide our true selves from others. The need to belong had been a constant in my life, and God began to show me that I did belong. I belonged to Him. I saw the truth of it all as He was restoring my soul. I wrote the apology, and I mailed the letter the next morning. I knew that within three days, he would receive the letter as long as he still lived at the address I had. Would I ever get a chance to explain why I reacted the way I did that night? I hoped so, but for now, at least he deserved an apology.

The next three days felt very long! Kyle did receive my letter. That evening, when he came home from work, he found a handwritten letter in his mailbox. My handwriting wasn't perfect, but my intentions were sincere. He kindly responded to me. He was able to find me on Facebook, and he sent me the kindest reply. As I read his reply, I began to shed those years of shame. His exact words were, "I never held that against you." Yes, I knew Kyle was a good man, but I was surprised to see those words. Wow, what a wonderful thing God had done in those three days. After exchanging messages, I asked him if we could be friends. His reply was "Friends has a good sound." I thanked him and told him how much I appreciated his kindness. I also told him maybe one day, over coffee, I could explain all that was going on in my life during that time.

So, what do you do after a moment like that? Well, girls call their friends! So, I called Gail. I had to talk to her! She knew 35 years ago that Kyle and I were meant to meet. She was my first call. When she answered, I told her everything that had just happened. Gail's expressions are priceless! She has this way of showing her feelings with a sigh that she holds out, like a little girl who just got her first pony. It's not loud; it's the sweetest sound, and I heard it coming through the phone lines as I shared the letter with her. She was amazed! She couldn't believe what she was hearing. I'm sure we were both crying, then laughing hysterically, then crying again, deeply over all those lost years. But we knew, we just knew God was up to something.

So, would there be a coffee date? I had no idea. Remember, I just needed to apologize, but sure, I hoped that I would see my "friend" again. I had some explaining to do. For a while, there was only silence, and I didn't talk to Kyle during this time. I did wish him a happy birthday when it came around. I wasn't going to miss that opportunity. A few months passed, and who do you think reached out for a coffee date? Yes, Kyle! We arranged a coffee date.

We hadn't talked on the phone or seen each other in thirty-five years, but the day he strolled up the sidewalk—while I was sitting across the street waiting—I recognized him right away. I knew it was him! Some things never change; he had a certain way of carrying himself when he walked, and that swagger was still there. I was sitting on a bench across the street with a bird's-eye view. Girls will be girls! He stopped at the coffee shop door, turned, and looked across the street. He saw me, turned again, and looked. I got up and walked across, smiling. We embraced and greeted each other with kind words. The coffee date lasted for hours. We had a wonderful time catching up on the past 35 years. He was a great listener. The evening ended with a nice dinner, and at the end of the night, I hugged him and thanked him for everything. I hurried to my car. My heart was happy but overwhelmed at the same time.

A few weeks later, Kyle sent me a text and asked if I would like to join him to visit Gail and her family. Since he was going to visit my friend, he thought I might enjoy coming along. Smooth, huh? I thought so too. Of course, I said yes—I would love that! This is a day my four sons will never forget, nor let me live it down. I hadn't dated anyone at this point, and I had never had a date pick me up at our house. My son, Blake, was home asleep when Kyle came to pick me up. My car was in the driveway, but I was so nervous I forgot to leave a note for Blake.

When we arrived at Gail's house, you can imagine the reunion. We went inside, I dropped my purse, and we all went outside to visit. Hours passed and thirty phone calls later, someone heard my phone ringing and came to get me. That's right, my four boys, who were now grown men, had been trying to find me all afternoon. They had no idea where I was! They saw my car in the driveway, but I was nowhere to be found. If I was on a date, they didn't know Kyle from Adam, and they were worried sick. It was awful! I knew they were right and felt terrible for what I put them through. They were men and were being protective.

I learned a valuable lesson that day! Sadly, I still had more lessons to learn because they felt the need to watch over me during this new season of my life. They knew how naive their mother could be at times. Fortunately, we got through it all, and now it has become a memory they love to remind me of—the day I received thirty phone calls and had them worried sick! God gave me four wonderful boys; they love me, and I am blessed.

We started dating after that day, and there was soon another "come to Jesus" moment. My boys wanted to meet this man, Kyle, saying, "Anyone that is going to be in our mother's life, we want to know him," exactly what one of my sons said on behalf of the others. You can only imagine the scene in my house as we gathered in my kitchen, with each of them questioning him. All four of them were priceless! I get tickled remembering that day. I felt so loved, and they made me proud! Kyle, well, he just took it like a man and answered every question kindly. He understood what they were doing and was up for the interrogation. I don't know exactly what broke the ice in that kitchen, but thankfully they laughed a lot, and we sat around the table for dinner that night. I'm sure, between the four of them, they knew all about Kyle before they even met him. Boys have their ways when it involves their mom! Most importantly, they liked him, and I had their approval.

After the day of 30 phone calls, Kyle and I were careful to update my boys until the newness of the relationship faded. We didn't mind; we understood. New chapters in life are scary for us and our kids. Even when we're grown, we're still afraid of change. I was facing the biggest change of my life. I enjoyed our dates, but I knew it would be a slow process. My home had become my refuge, a place where I knew God was with me.

Time passed, and I was still pinching myself over the miracle of my reunion with Kyle. We were great friends, but I loved him. Now, everything made sense. God had a plan 35 years ago; He knew exactly what I would go through and what I would need. Don't you just love God's timing?

We enjoyed dating, and my family loved him. We had been together for a while. I was doing what I do best—thinking in my own head, wondering what God is up to. Well, He let me know one Sunday morning through a song He inspired me to write. I grabbed my pen and paper and started to write these words. The chorus says, "It was all in God's plan, this woman and this man." Yes, He gave me this beautiful song titled "Second Chances." God revealed what was coming down the road to me; He whispered His plans in my ear. I pondered it in my heart for a long time and knew this was a song meant to be sung at a wedding. He provides a premonition and births a vision in our hearts. How can we move forward if we have nothing in front of us to see?

You can ask God to show you the vision He has for you! It was definitely a wedding song, a song meant for Kyle someday. I promise you, it's not easy to remarry at this age. I was nearly 60 years old! This was going to be difficult for me. Another reason

I wanted to write my story is to encourage you to keep going. If God presents it, He knows you better than you know yourself. He knows what He has planned for you, and He knows what you're capable of doing!

Kyle and I dated for two years, and we were very happy together. He made sure I was fully prepared, and he proposed to me. That's right, he waited until I was ready. I am grateful to him for that. He prayed and waited until that perfect moment arrived, and it did. The same front porch at his house out in the country, where we sat and got to know each other over those two years, is where he chose to propose. It was Mother's Day weekend! Such a meaningful weekend for him to propose because we used my mother's ring, which was very special to me, and now it has become part of my wedding ring. I still cherish that special moment with Kyle that night and the beautiful ring he had made just for me.

Our big day finally arrived, and the country club—where thirty-five years ago he took me on a date and I wanted to run—was the place we chose to get married. The venue was very special to Kyle. My oldest son, Hunter, officiated the ceremony, making it a meaningful part of us coming together as a family. All the children and grandchildren sat in the front row to witness and support us. We felt loved and blessed to have them all there. Choosing the music was easy. Two of my boys are musical artists in Nashville, and we selected songs they wrote. The songs fit us perfectly! It was a beautiful day for a wedding! Our families came together, embraced us, and each other.

One of the best parts of the day was our first dance as a married couple. Our life together was about to begin with that dance. My son, Jonathan, sang the song Kyle had chosen for us. The dance floor waited for the perfect note to start the music, and Kyle stepped onto it. He was waiting for me. The prayer I once said in the middle of a field as a young girl had been answered. Unconditional love between a man and a woman does exist! He gave me my heart's desire. He created love, and He wants us to experience it.

Unconditional love is something I witness every day in our home. Kyle is a wonderful man and my best friend. I feel blessed and loved more than I ever imagined possible. God truly exceeds anything we could ask or dream. He even hears the prayers from the heart of a young girl standing in a field. He is the God of second chances. He knew an apology letter would be perfect. Kyle and I were in awe and surprised by everything, but God wasn't. He had a plan that began developing 35 years earlier.

Jeremiah 1:5 says, "Before I formed you in the womb I knew you." No, God wasn't surprised. He planned it all long ago. Our lives are that important to Him, and He longs to fill us with His Word and fulfill our heart's desires. It was a beautiful moment that night as we danced together. God brought that dream to pass, and His words to me during that special moment were, "Dream on daughter, dream on!"

I Hope You Dance

The day at Topsail was winding down as we sat on the beach together, laughing and enjoying our time with family. It was a cooler day, but we didn't mind; we were happy to be there with our toes in the sand. It had been a wonderful day with family and friends. I knew we would be leaving soon, but I could feel the water calling me. So, I decided to tiptoe away from everyone and walk over to the water's edge. I love standing on the shore, staring out into the deep; it's a place to put things into perspective. God is so big, and it's where I go when I need to do just that.

As I walked over and looked down at the sand, I noticed it looked different today. There had been a lot of storms lately, but thankfully we were blessed with a sunny day. Interestingly, there wasn't a shell on the beach, and the grains of sand looked like millions of crystals. It was like a beautiful dance floor that glistened. They looked like brand-new grains of sand on the beach and, as they sparkled, they invited me to come and take a walk. For a moment, I thought I might be having a divine moment with the Father. I always hope for one. I turned and looked at everyone, and they seemed caught up in their conversations, so I decided to follow through and see where this moment was taking me. It is that still small voice that sometimes brings the most profound moments.

The waves splashed sporadically. Their ebbs and flows today were quite unusual. As I walked, the waves hit and the cold water splashed a little, and as the water receded to the ocean, this beautiful, glistening sand tugged at my heart, urging me to keep going. As I continued walking, I noticed my steps—they mimicked a little dance, and I chuckled, but I enjoyed it. The waves came and splashed just enough to tickle my legs, making me dance from the chill of the water on a glistening dance floor of sand. I looked around to see if anyone was watching me. I didn't want this moment to end. I was having fun alone, but then I realized something profound—I was having a divine moment, and I was not alone. I was dancing on the shores of Topsail with Jesus. He was the one beckoning me to come out. He wanted us to dance on that shimmering dance floor, just the two of us. My heart savored this special moment—a dance with Jesus before I leave this beautiful place. Our Father loves us that much! My heart swells, and my eyes glisten as I share this with you. Excitement awaits all of God's children if we just listen for Him.

As this happened, I began to count the years it had been. Eight years ago, I stood on the shores of Topsail Island as a broken woman, carrying so much loss in my heart. God wanted me to see what He could do in eight years. Remember the construction sign I shared earlier that said, "New Beginnings?" The number eight holds significance; it means new beginnings. It has been eight years, and today my feet feel light, burdens have been lifted, and my eyes glisten with joy and expectancy, like these grains of sand that glisten under my feet. He started right there and let the camera roll, revealing beauty and restoring my life. Now I feel joy in my heart as I danced with Jesus that day. I was reminded of His faithfulness to His daughter and how far He has brought me since that day eight years ago.

Jesus called me to the shoreline again. This time, it was to dance with Him in the same spot I found Him in my brokenness. As I took those small steps, I felt in my heart what Jesus can do for someone who trusts Him. Trust even when you're afraid. As I danced in the cold water, I realized I had no more tears; I could feel again, and joy was deep in my heart. Freedom wrapped itself around me, and it was a wonderful feeling. I am a woman I have never been before because I followed my heart and trusted in Jesus.

Dancing with Jesus is real. I hope you understand that dancing with Him is an intimate relationship with your Father. He desires a relationship with you. I wish that for you. I hope my story of dancing with Jesus restores your hope and vision. I encourage you to have the courage to take His hand and follow

Him. I pray my story of taking Jesus' hand and having the courage to dance will be the start of a great adventure for you. He will take you to places your heart longs to go. Jesus is the lover of your soul, and you will see just how romantic He can be, with miracles awaiting you.

I followed my heart this morning and took a drive to the place I felt called to write this final chapter. I opened my sunroof and let the sunshine in. It is a beautiful day, and I feel incredible. There's a beautiful song playing, "Let it Happen," by United Pursuit. The lyrics are "Take me back, back to the beginning, when I was young and running through the fields with you."[1]

God knew you before you were formed in the womb. You entered this world as a child of God, and there is a place where you and God ran together. If you have drifted away, He wants you to know He longs for you. Remember the Psalm that was so dear to my mother's heart? She wrote Psalm 139 beside her signature on every letter I ever received from her. It especially seems fitting today as I write the final words of Dancing with Jesus: "How precious also are thy thoughts unto me, O God! How great is the sum of them! If I should count them, they are more in number than the sand; when I awake, I am still with thee."[2] You are always in the heart and mind of God; He thinks of you in every circumstance of your life. Please do yourself a favor and meditate on every word of this Psalm — see how much He loves you, and believe it. If I should count His thoughts towards me, they are more in number than the sand. When you spend time in God's Word, you will be changed.

I have enjoyed entering your world as you have entered mine. I want to thank you for taking the time for both of us. You matter! God wants you to know that! Lastly, more than anything, I hope you dance. When you hear His still, small voice, follow Him because the world is waiting to see the masterpiece that you are. Dance with Him!

***

Scan to listen to Lori's song, "I Want to Dance with You Jesus"

Acknowledgements

Writing *Dancing with Jesus* has been one of the most profound experiences of my life, and I could not have done it alone. God surrounded me with an extraordinary circle of love—my family, friends, and encouragers—who held me up, believed in me, and reminded me of God's faithfulness when I needed it most. This is for all of you who stood beside me—thank you for helping me step into my calling with boldness and joy.

To my husband, Kyle—my best friend and the love of my life—you have shown me unconditional love and the freedom to become all God created me to be. Thank you, honey. It means more than you will ever know. In the miracle of you and me, I gained a daughter. I love you very much.

To my four boys, I love you so much. I cherish being your mother. I treasure every moment—teaching you, caring for you, and praying over you. You have brought me immeasurable joy, and I am overwhelmed by the great men of God you have become. The plans God has for each of you leave me in awe. As Isaiah 49:18 so beautifully says, "You are jewels around my neck." In the words of your Ganny, "I love you sooooooooooo much!"

To my girls, Kristen, Nicole, and Jessica—you are my heart. God handpicked each of you, and I am blessed beyond measure. You are unique, beautiful, and forever cherished. I love you.

To my wonderful, playful, and captivating eight grandchildren—my world comes alive in your presence! I can't wait to see all that God will do in and through you. Hold tight to your child-like faith—it will carry you all your days. You are so precious to me.

To my brother and sister-in-love, Todd and Ren, and your beautiful family—thank you, thank you, thank you! You never gave up on me. You lifted my arms when I was weary and believed when I couldn't. I love you deeply.

To my dear friend Doris—you have walked with me through so much pain and always met me with a Scripture and love. From the time I was a young girl, you revealed God's love to me, and I never forgot it. Your life is proof that one person can make an eternal difference. I love you.

To my Uncle George and Aunt Diane, I'm so grateful for your prayers and unwavering support. I always knew I could call on you. Thank you for being there. I love you.

To my Daddy—I always wanted to be your little girl. I didn't get that chance, and I've made peace with that. I've learned that until a wound heals, pain begets pain. But in His mercy, the Father used that pain to bring healing—not just to me, but through me to others. And in all of it, He whispered that I was His little girl all along. I love you, Daddy.

To my beautiful Mom—every book I ever write will always have a place for you. Your example as a mother will live on in my heart forever. If I could write another book, it would be about you—the way you touched lives in our town and everywhere you went. I pray you can see the answers to your prayers unfolding. You were the best Mother and Ganny anyone could ask for. I love you dearly and miss you always.

And finally, Lovell and Fran—you were a true Godsend at just the right time. Lovell, thank you for befriending me that special evening. Your genuine interest and the words you poured into me changed everything. To both of you—thank you for believing in my story and for choosing to publish my book. Your editing, encouragement, and investment have made *Dancing with Jesus* what it is. There are no words strong enough to express my gratitude. Thank you from the bottom of my heart.

***

A Special Note to You, Dear Reader

As you turn these pages, I pray you feel seen, known, and deeply loved by the One who dances over you with joy. You may have picked up this book searching for answers, hope, or healing—and I want you to know, you are not alone. Every word was written with you in mind, wrapped in prayer, and inspired by a God who never stops pursuing you.

May Dancing with Jesus be more than just a book—it is my prayer that it becomes a moment of encounter for you. A reminder that no matter where you've been, no matter what you've faced, you are invited into a divine rhythm of grace, healing, and joy. And if you're still waiting on your miracle—don't stop dancing. Jesus is right there with you.

With love and hope,
Lori

About the author

Lori Michalina Wood is a dedicated Christian author, speaker, and mother, whose life and writing reflect her journey of faith, healing, and restoration. Born with a deep-seated trust in God, Lori accepted Christ at a young age. Her debut book, *The Invitation: A Love Story* (published July 18, 2022), is a heartfelt memoir of her encounters with God's grace and purpose through difficult trials. In it, she invites readers to step out of fear and insecurity—"out of the misty lowlands...onto a walk that is on a much higher plain"—as she shares how her faith carried her from sorrow and tragedy to becoming an "oak of righteousness" sustained by God's love.

The Invitation is Lori's testimony of trusting in God during deep waters and finding freedom from lies of rejection and unworthiness. Throughout, she offers readers a path toward spiritual renewal—emphasizing that, through Christ, we receive "beauty for ashes, joy for mourning, and a garment of praise instead of a spirit of despair".

Lori resides in a small North Carolina community with her husband, Kyle McClintock. She enjoys being a mother to four boys and a grandmother. Her beloved Australian puppy, Bogey, brings her lots of joy. She continues her writing with *Dancing with Jesus*, the sequel to *The Invitation*. When she's not writing or caring for her family, she finds peace and inspiration walking along the serene shores of Topsail Island. Her life is a portrait of unwavering faith, rooted in family and coastal tranquility.

Endnotes

His Majesty

1. Mark 10:14

2. Psalm 121:1-3

3. Psalm 139:13-14

The Misty Lowlands

1. A.W. Tozer, *The Pursuit of God* (Camp Hill, PA: Christian Publications, 1982)

2. Genesis 3:1-6

3. 1 Samuel 17:1-50

4. 1 Samuel 17:34-37, 45-50

5. 1 Samuel 17:50-51

6. Exodus 3:1-22; 4:1-17

7. Psalm 77:16-20

8. Psalm 18:19

The Dance Floor

1. *Shall We Dance*, directed by Peter Chelsom (Miramax Films, 2004)

2. *Dancing with the Stars*, created by BBC Worldwide Productions, premiered June 1, 2005, on ABC

3. *Footloose*, directed by Herbert Ross (Paramount Pictures, 1984)

4. Ecclesiastes 3:1–4, as quoted in *Footloose*, directed by Herbert Ross (Paramount Pictures, 1984)

5. Psalm 46:10

6. *The Wizard of Oz*, directed by Victor Fleming (Metro-Goldwyn-Mayer, 1939), spoken by Dorothy, Tin Man, and Scarecrow

7. Joshua 10:13

8. The word *mesa* comes from Spanish, meaning "table." In geography, it refers to an elevated area of land with a flat top and steep sides, resembling a table. This term is often used in pastoral imagery to describe tablelands where shepherds lead their flocks.

9. Matthew 18:3

10. 2 Corinthians 12:9

You Belong to Me

1. Dean Martin, *You Belong to Me*, performed by Dean Martin, Capitol Records, 1952. Written by Chilton Price, Pee Wee King, and Redd Stewart

2. Caroline Leaf, *Switch On Your Brain: The Key to Peak Happiness, Thinking, and Health* (Baker Books, 2013)

3. Matthew 18:3

4. Adelaide A. Pollard, *Have Thine Own Way, Lord*, 1907. Lyrics by Adelaide A. Pollard; music by George C. Stebbins

5. Brené Brown, *Braving the Wilderness: The Quest for True Belonging and the Courage to Stand Alone* (New York: Random House, 2017)

6. Dean Martin, *You Belong to Me*, performed by Dean Martin, Capitol Records, 1952

Dancing with Jesus

1. John and Stasi Eldredge, *Captivating: Unveiling the Mystery of a Woman's Soul* (Nashville: Thomas Nelson, 2005)

2. Jeremiah 29:11

3. Isaiah 43:2

4. Ernie Haase & Signature Sound, *Walking Through Fire*, written by Devin McGlamery, Lee Black & Sue C. Smith; released on Clear Skies (StowTown Records, 2018)

Cinderella's Castle

1. *Beauty and the Beast*. Directed by Gary Trousdale and Kirk Wise, Walt Disney Pictures, 1991

2. See Matthew 27:33, Mark 15:22, Luke 23:33, and John 19:17 for biblical accounts of Jesus' crucifixion at Golgotha, also known as "the place of the skull"

3. *Walt Disney's Cinderella*, directed by Clyde Geronimi, Wilfred Jackson, and Hamilton Luske (Burbank, CA: Walt Disney Productions, 1950), spoken by the Fairy Godmother

Back to the Garden

1. United Pursuit, *Let It Happen*, Simple Gospel, United Pursuit Records, 2015

2. A.W. Tozer, *The Pursuit of God* (Camp Hill, PA: Christian Publications, 1982), paraphrased from themes in Chapter 1, "Following Hard After God"

3. Luke 22:42

4. Genesis 1:1-2

5. Genesis 1:3

6. Genesis 1:4

7. Matthew 26:36-46

8. Matthew 26:39

9. John 11:25-26

10. Genesis 15:1-6

11. 2 Corinthians 4:4

The Life of the Eagle

1. Richard L. Evans, *Life of the Eagle*, Archebooks Pub, 2004

2. Matthew 28:6-7

3. Mark 10:46-48

4. Mark 5:25-34

5. Isaiah 40:31

It's Time

1. Psalm 16:7

2. John 10:27

3. Luke 1:26-38; Luke 2:19

4. Ecclesiastes 7:3

5. Genesis 3:1-6

6. Hosea 2:16

7. Hosea 2:19

Forty Minutes vs. Forty Days

1. Matthew 5:44; Luke 6:27-28

2. 1 John 1:9

3. 1 Samuel 17:45

4. Mark 8:35

5. Matthew 1:22-23

You Know My Name

1. "You Know My Name," written by Brenton Brown, Jimi Cravity, and Tasha Cobbs Leonard. Performed by Tasha Cobbs Leonard. © 2017 Motown Gospel

2. Psalm 139:2, 4, 16

3. Paraphrased from Isaiah 43:2

Dancing in the Dark

1. Paraphrased from Exodus 14:16

2. Genesis 15-18

3. Genesis 16:1-4, 17:15-19, 18:9-15, and 21:1-3

4. Genesis 22:1-4

5. Romans 5:8

6. Genesis 22:12-18

7. Genesis 22:1-12

8. Proverbs 4:23

Hindsight is 20/20

1. Hebrews 11:1

2. "Amazing Grace," lyrics by John Newton, 1779. Public domain

Breaking or Becoming

1. Strong's H8492

2. Isaiah 43:18-19

Salty Coffee

1. Luke 7:36-50

2. Luke 7:36-50

3. John 10:10

4. Ecclesiastes 2:26

5. Jeremiah 15:16

6. Isaiah 61:2-3

7. A.W. Tozer, *The Pursuit of God* (Camp Hill, PA: Christian Publications, 1948)

8. Psalm 16:11

9. Psalm 23:2

Turn North

1. *The Wizard of Oz*, directed by Victor Fleming, performances by Judy Garland and Frank Morgan, Metro-Goldwyn-Mayer, 1939

2. Deuteronomy 2:3

3. Exodus 14:13

4. Exodus 4:22-23

5. Nehemiah 2:17

6. Howard Thurman, *The Living Wisdom of Howard Thurman: A Visionary for Our Time*, edited by Walter Earl Fluker (Berrett-Kochler Publishers, 2006)

The Unveiling

1. Genesis 2:18-23

2. John and Stasi Eldredge, *Captivating: Unveiling the Mystery of a Woman's Soul* (Nashville: Thomas Nelson, 2005)

3. Proverbs 23:7

4. Proverbs 4:23

5. A.W. Tozer, *The Pursuit of God* (Camp Hill, PA: Christian Publications, 1982)

6. Psalm 121

7. Numbers 10:9

8. Pierre Teilhard de Chardin, as quoted in *The Phenomenon of Man* (1955). Though this exact phrasing may not appear verbatim in his writings, it summarizes themes found throughout his work.

9. https://www.youtube.com/watch?v=JojzZGvdDIM

10. Psalm 139:13

11. *My Big Fat Greek Wedding*, directed by Joel Zwick, written by Nia Vardalos, IFC Films, 2002

I Hope You Dance

1. United Pursuit. *Let It Happen*. From the album Simple Gospel, 2015. © United Pursuit Music

2. Psalm 139:17-18